SALESpeak

SALESpeak

Everybody Sells Something

....

A '90s Guide to Creating Memorable & Persuasive Presentations

by
TERRI SJODIN

THE SUMMIT PUBLISHING GROUP, ARLINGTON, TEXAS

The Summit Publishing Group
1112 East Copeland Road, Fifth Floor
Arlington, Texas 76011

99 98   5 4 3 2

Library of Congress Cataloging-in-Publication Data
Sjodin, Terri L.
    SALESpeak : everybody sells something / by Terri L. Sjodin.
        p. cm.
    ISBN 1-56530-192-7 (hard cover)
    1. Business presentations. 2. Public speaking. 3. Business communication. I. Title.
HF5718.22.S58 1995b
658.4'52–dc20   95-40546
                                                                    CIP

Book design by David Sims

▼

To my parents,

Jan and Pete Sjodin

▲

SALESpeak # Contents

Chapter 3
Listening Communication Skills   35
••

Chapter 4
Persuasive Speaking: The Career Enhancer   43
••

Chapter 5
Tools of the Trade

Chapter 6
How to Build a Great Presentation   83

Chapter 7
Becoming a Power Speaker   105

Preface

When I look back at my years in school and at the public education system in general, I realize how fortunate I am to have had a high school speech coach who encouraged me to begin training in the "art" of public speaking. If I hadn't, I would probably find myself in an altogether different career.

It was only after I was graduated from college that I realized the advantage I had because of my training in debate and public speaking. I was more effective in selling my ideas and myself than many of my contemporaries. These skills are critical in job interviews and are reflected in sales commission checks and in promotions.

I did not want to go into sales originally. I did so partly because it was the only job I could find at the time. I had studied one-on-one and group presentations, as well as small-group dynamics, and I was able to adapt to a selling environment.

As I traveled nationwide making business presentations, the surprising thing I noticed was how people seemed to encounter difficulty when communicating information. More startling, this observation proved as true for sales professionals as it did for anyone else. It was the area where most business people revealed their greatest deficiency. For many, it was not that they didn't know what to say, it was that they couldn't deliver the information in a format that was polished, professional, and–most importantly–persuasive. Many felt they would sound neither dynamic nor convincing, and the result was that they never tried.

While I was selling appearance dates for seminar talks by other national speakers, my clients would come up to me and say,

"Terri, if I could speak the way you do, I could sell anything."
People wanted to know how I learned to deliver such strong presentations. I told them it related to my training in public speaking. When I mentioned public speaking classes to sales managers,
however, they said, "No, we're not going to sign up for public
speaking training. That's not what we do." The irony was, public
speaking really was what they did, but they didn't realize it since
their typical audience was only one or two people.

I began to wonder what the response would be if we designed
a public speaking program just for sales professionals. How would
salespeople respond if we could devote all training exclusively to
the delivery portion of the sales call? Creating a program that
would help sales professionals become stronger presenters, by giving them polish and the ability to sound highly persuasive, would
undoubtedly help their sales. Then it struck me: Everybody sells
something—not just those in the sales and marketing professions!
For example, firemen, architects, local politicians, and teachers all
sell ideas. Even plumbers sell goods and services to the public.

I developed my first program and called it The Power of
Public Speaking for Today's Sales Professional. The presentations
each drew fifty or sixty people, not enough to be economically
viable. The sales professionals who came were impressed, however, and said, "Wow, this is great. I've never had a class like this
before." But still we could not get the attendance up.

Then a mentor, Floyd Wickman, said to me, "Terri, if public
speaking is the number one fear among most individuals, why
would you want to put that in your title? That phrase 'public
speaking' scares people to death. Why don't you just change the
title and I bet you will get more people to attend."

So I changed the title to The Art of Selling, It's All in Your
Delivery. Immediately, we doubled our attendance. Even with
our new title, though, it was a challenging sell during those early
months because nobody ever had done anything like it before.
There are many training companies teaching public speaking, but

none focus specifically on the job of the sales professional. All address how to speak before groups. Salespeople typically don't speak to groups. Their time is spent in one-on-one presentations with their clients or in making prospecting calls. Whether people are making a call to set appointments or delivering small group presentations, they use public speaking techniques.

My fledgling company, Sjodin Communications, started by offering a lecture-only seminar. That was a four-and-a-half-hour program to get people thinking about augmenting their personal training and development agenda. We wanted people to consider a public speaking course that applied specifically to their line of work.

The next step was to design activity workshops. I videotaped each salesperson's presentation and played it back so they could hear and see themselves as others do. Once people saw how they were communicating, they were able to find weak points that needed to be strengthened.

After about a year-and-a-half of traveling nationwide and speaking to professionals from a variety of different industries—everyone from cosmetics consultants to computer engineers—I realized a lot of people were coming to hear the presentations who weren't necessarily in sales. Once again my observation was verified that, no matter what people do for a living, everybody sells something.

The book brings together a vast array of experiences so anyone reading it can benefit from those who have already gone through the training. The book teaches the basic principles of public speaking as they relate to what a sales professional does on a daily basis—what we all do in many ways each day.

By publishing this book I hope to accomplish several things. The overall intent is to help people become more effective communicators. I hope to achieve that aim by providing them with the means to deliver more polished, persuasive, and effective presentations.

Say you want to do more than deliver a "canned" presentation or use memorized closes—this book will show you how to make your presentation sound natural and persuasive. How do I make my talk sound polished and flowing? How do I build a case for why someone should work with me or my company? These are the questions asked by people who want to ascend to the next phase in their careers.

With polish and the ability to be persuasive, people become more confident. They are more successful because with stronger communications skills they build stronger relationships with their clients or their employees. I hope this book will also contribute to managers and other professionals who may want to improve their ability to communicate their ideas to their colleagues.

Perhaps after reading this book, people will be less apt to get tense when hearing the words "public speaking." All of us do a lot of public speaking—we just don't like to acknowledge it. We might as well face the fact that there is a marriage between public speaking and sales, and that the true matchmakers are sales professionals.

Achieving self-improvement and change is possible and exciting. I have made it my personal commitment to stay in the industry and to keep helping people realize improvement. When one looks at the before-and-after tapes from training workshops, the changes in student accomplishment are dramatic. After a little practice, people start to have fun. It doesn't take long; it just takes commitment and a little effort. Everybody can do it.

We will continue to offer the lecture-only seminars and the workshops and will make every effort to update this book to meet current market requirements.

On a final note, I would like to encourage parents to use this book as the basis for teaching their children how to become more effective communicators. Consider exposing your children to public speaking early as a means of preventing their fear of it later on in life. Possessing public speaking skills can provide a tremendous advantage to their success in an increasingly complex adult world.

Thank you for including *SALESpeak: Everybody Sells Something* in your personal development library. I know the information in this book will provide you with the most useful tools available for furthering your career, whether it be in sales or another profession.

Terri L Sjodin

Ack

Acknowledgments

The material in this book is the collective wisdom of many individuals and the result of numerous contacts I have had with astute teachers and experienced business people during the past fifteen years. It is the result of meeting individuals who have a special ability to help others achieve their dreams. If I can help another achieve his or her own dream, I will be headed along the road toward returning the favors bestowed on me.

To complete a book means you first have to start it, and none are more responsible for that beginning than my parents, Jan and Pete Sjodin. They have given me constant love and support and from the start have shown a sincere interest in my career. They have instilled in me a sound belief in myself and in my dreams. I also would like to express my gratitude to my grandmother, Doris Burns, who continues to inspire me to "perform," and my sister Kim, who was always there to provide backup at trade shows and overall encouragement when I needed help most.

No company can be successful without effective support, and my national coordinator, friend, and trusted confidant, Mary Jo Standley, has worked long, hard hours in the background to make certain that we met our goals and our commitments. Her devoted efforts have helped make it possible to take Sjodin Communications to the next level.

Chris Smith of CC Communications in Long Beach, California, who assisted me in compiling this material and whose commitment and editorial skills have made publication of this book possible, has my sincere thanks.

My high school speech coach, Jim Caforio, truly taught me the art of delivery, and my college coach, Peg Taylor, taught me the importance of doing research and how to build a persuasive presentation. I extend my heartfelt appreciation to both of these outstanding instructors.

A mentor and friend who has always been available to listen to my ideas and offer insightful feedback is Jerry Anderson. His wisdom, encouragement, and support have provided a vital foundation for my business planning.

Richard Bitner, who helped Sjodin Communications to grow during a period when other businesses were failing, deserves my compliments and has my thanks and best wishes for the future. And special thanks must go to Larry Reese, Nick Taylor, Ryan Kelly, Greg Dell, Jason Tillery, and Janice Gaski who are always willing to help. I am blessed to have friends like them.

I would also like to express my appreciation to the hundreds of corporations and individuals whose sales managers and executives have sponsored my training seminars and workshops during the past four years. We will continue to work hard to earn and maintain your business.

Terri L. Sjodin

Chapter 1

SALESpeak

Persuasive Public Speaking

I f you are like most business or professional people, you are constantly looking for opportunities to further your career and increase your income. Even if you are locked into regular annual raises, you know you could earn a little more just by being promoted or maybe changing jobs. Although your skills are first class, it is likely that someone else less qualified is seizing opportunities you would like to be yours.

The difference between profiting from those opportunities and missing them is often the ability to sell yourself and your ideas. Whether you are an engineer, a fireman, a teacher, or a sales professional, the ability to persuade individuals to believe you, and then act on what you are saying, is a critical element of your success. It is central to your economic well-being. No matter who you are, you have something to sell. Frequently in the course of your career you will be called upon to sell something—especially yourself.

Perhaps engineers constitute the least sales- and promotion-oriented group I know. Engineers like to rely on facts, numbers, and technology to lead people toward making the right decisions. However, if you need to convince the company president, or your supervisor, why a project needs more funding, additional engineering assistants, or even more time, you have a selling job ahead of you.

The most common form of selling today may be simply finding a job. Even firefighters have to go through a series of in-depth interviews in which they are probed on why they should be selected over hundreds of other candidates who are applying for the same position. These men and women have to explain why they would benefit the department. This process is repeated every time they seek a promotion—all the way up to the job of chief.

Whether you are applying for a college internship or your first job out of school, you have to know how to sell yourself and your ideas. Just getting in the door for an interview frequently requires that you justify why people should bother to talk with you.

Whether you are applying for a college internship or your first job out of school, you have to know how to sell yourself and your ideas.

If you are a sales professional, you understand that the selling process doesn't begin with your formal presentation. It starts much earlier when you are trying to get in the door of the prospective client. Knowing effective ways to explain how you can be of service to the company can get you a critical appointment with the manager.

I was working for the Achievement Group in 1987 representing professional speakers widely known for their ability to clearly communicate new and effective sales techniques. My job was to sell these speakers to corporate clients who needed to train and motivate their sales professionals.

My first territory included a large residential real estate organization. Headed by a man named Jim _____, it was a highly successful group with nine offices, each having more than fifty agents. My goal was to deliver a group presentation to their sales staff. Management policy, however, prevented outside salespeople from giving presentations during staff meetings.

The implied closed-door approach frustrated me, particularly for a sales organization, and it also stimulated my competitive imagination. I asked myself how I could possibly go around this restriction, but my colleagues continued to discourage me.

When I asked other, more experienced salesmen from the Achievement Group team what they would suggest I do, they responded: "Forget it, Terri, you will never get in there. It is a closed office. Move on to the next account."

Now, what is the difference between a closed office and an open office? (I have never entered an office that was posted, "Open to Vendors and Solicitors.") The answer is, there is no difference, except for the amount of time it takes to get through the door.

I followed up anyway with phone calls and mailings, but nothing happened. I changed my strategy and began meeting with each manager separately, but every one of them said the same thing: If I wanted to get into the offices, I would have to have permission from Jim. So I turned my attention toward getting an appointment with him. No such luck. He had a very good secretary, one who had been trained to screen calls from salespeople.

The more rejection I got, the more interested I became in getting inside their organization. I was beginning to realize just how difficult it was. I surmised that few, if any, training sales agents had given presentations to these people. If I could get inside, I knew it would be a great account.

The movie *Wall Street* gave me the inspiration I needed. In the movie, the lead character, played by Charlie Sheen, delivers a box of imported cigars to his prospect on his birthday. I decided I could come up with one of the "creative solutions" characterized in the film. I decided to buy a long-stemmed white rose and resolved to deliver it to Jim in person. I felt a white rose was appropriate because it symbolized integrity (in addition to the fact that I was poor and my company didn't provide salespeople with expense accounts).

The only appropriate place that I could think to approach him was in the parking lot outside his office. So at 5:30 A.M. I took up sentry duty next to his car stall, which was clearly marked with his name. After I had waited about an hour and a half, a car pulled up. Its driver was obviously the man I had come to find.

"Excuse me, are you Jim _____?" I asked timidly, but somewhat reassured by the fact that I had on my best suit.

"Yes, I'm Jim. Who wants to know?"

"Just some young gal who needs about ten minutes of your time," I replied.

"What is she selling?" he asked, cutting to the chase.

"I don't suppose she is selling anything," I said, deferring the obvious. "I think she just needs to deliver this flower."

The laughter that crossed his lips was a great relief. He opened the card that I had included with my gift. It read: "Mr. _____, please just give me ten minutes of your time. I definitely believe I have something that will be of interest to you."

"I don't have ten minutes," he said. "You have two minutes as we walk from this car to that door."

Every debating technique I had learned in college sprang to readiness. I came up with more reasons in two minutes for why he would be at risk if he didn't meet with me than I had used in the last three months with all my other clients. My degree in speech communications paid off. I knew instinctively how to build my presentation and deliver it.

"Okay," he said. "I'll give you your ten minutes. Come back tomorrow at nine o'clock." I kept to his schedule and delivered my presentation in ten minutes. However, our meeting lasted one and a half hours. What exceeded my most exaggerated hopes was his sending a letter of recommendation to each of his managers telling them why they should let me make a presentation to their staffs. He was, by this time, convinced that it was essential for his agents to hear the story I had to tell. If they could adopt the sales posture that I was promoting, he knew that his organization would be enhanced.

On another level, however, his cooperation came down to something more basic—and more personal. I believe it was a direct result of my giving him the rose and doing so before anyone else was up and working that morning. It wasn't an expensive perk. It was just a simple thing that made him think that I believed he was special and that I was willing to be creative and work harder to earn his business. There is a big difference between buying business and earning business. Creative thinking can make a big difference in your gaining access to people. Once you have grabbed their attention, you can support your position by delivering a solid, professional presentation.

When you finish this book, I hope you will think of the white rose. I hope you will practice your public speaking skills with passion, and I hope you will develop the habit of presenting your ideas in a logical way formulated to generate action in what is unquestionably a competitive marketplace. Make a commitment! Miracles don't happen with an explosion and flash of light. They start out like a small snowball rolling downhill. Little changes become magnified over time. Today is the best time to start your personal journey toward what can be truly a miraculous future. To deliver dynamic presentations, we must learn to combine hustle with polish, persuasion, and uniqueness.

What Is Persuasive Public Speaking?

We are all salesmen and saleswomen at one time or another during the course of a day, working to get an idea accepted by a group or individual. Teachers sell their students on the value of becoming educated and learning new material. A butcher persuades a customer to select a certain cut of choice meat. We paint a picture of the menu of a new Italian restaurant across town we want our co-workers to try for lunch. In each case, we are giving persuasive talks, though we may not be aware of it. For those of us who make our living in sales, 80 percent of our time is spent communicating. Do we think of ourselves as public speakers? Certainly not! We would rather tame snakes than stand in front of our peers to give a speech. Surveys show that public speaking is our single most feared activity. Yet, how do we spend most of our days? In public speaking activities—we just don't like to think we do. We depend on our speaking skills to share our "messages" clearly and with credibility, whether we are speaking on the telephone one-on-one or delivering small group talks.

Persuasive public speaking is a learned activity. It is the application of formal principles of effective public speaking to the sales presentation. It is a new marriage between the strict principles found in the speech departments of our nation's college classrooms and the fascinating kaleidoscopic world of vendor sales. It is a way to compete in the lean 1990s and to ensure ourselves of being on top of every element within our control, as we address our peers with ideas that need their decisions. It is the combination necessary to ensure our presentation has both excellent content and outstanding delivery. It is a way to make what we say credible and, most important, to make us unique.

Who Should Read This Book?

This book is written for business and professional people as well as for those in the selling profession. It assumes a rudimentary knowledge of sales technique. It is ironic that many sales professionals, before they are sent into the field, are given precious little training. They are given more information than they or their customers would ever want to know about their products. They are briefed with videos and other colorful media about the company's founding and subsequent expansion, and they always are showed how to complete an order form. Frequently, however, that is the extent of their sales training. They either sink or swim.

This book is a refinement of the basic art of selling, and it is presumed that, if your early training was similar to that just described, you have learned to swim. Get set, because you now are going to learn how to swim in a race!

This book also is for anyone who gives one-on-one presentations, whether a company manager, a teacher, or a community volunteer. A speech doesn't require a large audience. It can be, and often is, delivered to an individual. If you want to know how to become more effective at selling your ideas—and who doesn't—you will learn a great deal by reading this book. For people who prize their careers and realize the critical importance of being able to communicate their ideas as a means to promotion, *SALESpeak: Everybody Sells Something* will be a resource. Effective public speaking is the measure of every modern executive.

To appreciate just how important public speaking skills are today, think of the 1992 presidential election in which independent Ross Perot attracted a large number of voters who were disillusioned with the two traditional parties. In spite of his independent status, Perot posed a serious challenge to both incumbent Republican President George Bush and Democratic candidate Bill Clinton. A factor in the campaign, however, was a series of debates between the leading candidates and another involving their vice-presidential running mates. Unfortunately for Perot, his selection for vice-president was not a dazzling public speaker.

Vice Admiral James Stockdale was a highly respected Vietnam War hero and an accomplished military executive, but he was not a strong presenter. Viewers who saw the debates will never forget the point at which Stockdale began fiddling with his hearing aid, stopping the talks dead and creating the impression, albeit erroneous, that he was too old to run for the nation's second highest office. Polls taken afterward showed that imperfections in Stockdale's style and delivery gave undecided voters the reason they needed to discount the Perot ticket altogether. Instead they moved on to the task of deciding between the two major candidates. If Stockdale had possessed the public speaking skills of Clinton's running mate, Senator Al Gore, it is possible the outcome of the election would have been altogether different.

The interesting thing to remember is that Stockdale's sterling qualifications earned him a *chance* at high office, but they were not the deciding factors. He had to demonstrate in person to voters that he was qualified and convince them they would be making the right choice if they relied on him and his running mate.

We might think of the debates as a sort of national public job interview. That idea suggests to me that any job applicant who thinks a résumé alone, without benefit of a convincing oral presentation, will secure a corporate position is apt to be looking for work for quite some time.

Among all the people who will benefit from this book, I have one particular reader in mind from start to finish: the goal-setter who wants to be the best salesperson that he or she can become. To you go my compliments for wanting to achieve a level of personal fulfillment through excellence. I believe that aiming to be a great salesperson means aiming to be a great public speaker and presenter.

Why Is This Book Timely?

During the 1980s, there was a reaction against the image of the pushy salesperson, the "doorknob-style" hard closer (who reaches for the doorknob as if to leave, thereby temporarily lowering the prospect's resistance). The words "integrity" and "honesty" became important to the many dedicated, hardworking professionals who chose sales as their career path. Along with this post-Watergate emphasis on ethics came a concomitant level of prosperity. These two influences combined to provide a climate in which salespeople were able to survive, even prosper, without ever becoming effective closers. They became providers of information; the more the better. Just give the client tons of information, and eventually, the client was sure to buy something. Generally, they would. It was pleasant for salespeople, really. But now things have changed. In the 1990s, we can't just provide information and obtain the client's business. Why? Because we never hear the word "no" when all we do is disseminate information. The only trouble is, we don't hear the word "yes" either.

The marketplace has changed, and, compared to the previous decade, the 1990s already are proving to be a whole new ballgame for the sales professional. It is a lean market (in case you hadn't noticed), and people are not engaging in sales encounters for entertainment. They are shopping harder than ever. You can bet they are checking up to five different suppliers before they make a decision. What they actually may be shopping for, however, is the right salesperson. What they often are looking for more than the lowest price is the best value. Only a salesperson can lead them into making an informed decision when it comes to value. The salesperson who has the most polished and believable presentation, the best argument supported by the strongest facts,

▼

The marketplace has changed, and, compared to the previous decade, the 1990s already are proving to be a whole new ballgame for the sales professional.

▲

is the one who will be perceived as offering the greatest value. People will spend more money to work with those they like and will reject working with those they don't like, even if it is cheaper to do so.

It is the perception of value that counts. The client has to perceive your presentation as effective, your product or service as worthwhile. Just providing information makes you just like your competitor—and it doesn't mean that you are selling. There is no sense of urgency in an informative presentation. You may feel comfortable giving such an informative talk, but ask yourself, why? The reason you feel comfortable is because you never hear the word "no" when all you do is disseminate information.

Why Is This Book Unique?

As far as I am aware, no one has taken the principles of speech communication as taught in the academic environment and applied them to sales. There are many books on public speaking and numerous books on sales. There are plenty that tell you what to say. This one teaches you how to say it. It teaches public speaking skills, then applies them to your specific sales presentation.

It may be appropriate here to recognize the contribution of the cadre of entertaining and effective salespeople who, without a formal curriculum, learned public speaking techniques on their own with the intent of applying them to their sales activities. They are the profession's mentors and frequently the top producers in their fields. With a little practice, you too can develop dazzling presentations that are truly memorable. While each of us is blessed with a different level of talent, speaking ability is a learned skill. So do not think for a minute that you "either have it or you don't." You can learn it.

What Will You Learn?

Here is a list of twenty-six topics that I will cover. You will be familiar with them all by the time you have finished the book.

1. The four major elements of a sale
2. How to implement your previously learned techniques
3. How to become "memorable" to your clients
4. How to move a prospect to action
5. The effect of the "three-to-five-company" rule

6. The significance of the "80-20 Rule" in today's market
7. Five critical listening skills
8. Three major types of presentations
9. Four speaking formats
10. How to evaluate your audience
11. Five sales elements you can control
12. How to use "signposting"
13. The overnight presentation
14. Eight major speech supports to gain credibility
15. How to develop a creative sales imagination
16. The refinements to become a "power speaker"
17. Eight causes of "speaker's fright"
18. The "dos and don'ts" when nervous
19. Skill-builders to improve your voice
20. Creating a lasting impression
21. Controlling nonverbal communication
22. Five logical steps to persuasion
23. Twelve emotional factors that move prospects toward commitment
24. Twenty-one keys to a powerful style
25. The proper and improper uses of visual aids
26. How to do a self-critique

What Must You Overcome?

In order to become a more effective salesperson and a dazzling public speaker, there are several things you will likely have to overcome. The biggest one is fear. Survey respondents cite speaking before a group as the activity they fear and dread most. I will share with you ideas on how to channel your fear into energy through identifying its causes.

If you have been giving presentations already, you may have to overcome a few habits which are deeply ingrained.

Relinquishing these can be difficult when we perceive them as part of our personalities.

To improve our presentation means to set higher goals for ourselves. We must give up our comfortable attitude of "just getting by." Giving a solid, persuasive talk is challenging. If it were easy, everyone would be doing it. One reason why it can be so rewarding is that everyone is not doing it, and we can shine by comparison. So we must overcome the inertia keeping us from accomplishing what is admittedly a challenge but is also a simple fact of life on the road to self-improvement.

Each of us must also overcome the perception that he or she is someone who is unable to give a public speech. Being able to give a dazzling, persuasive presentation is a learned skill. Recognize that you already spend 80 percent of your time communicating. You can do it, so make a commitment. Ironically, those of us who depend on our communication skills the most are the last to admit we frequently give "speeches." We may not recognize the one-on-one talk or small group presentation as being a speech. However, a speech is a presentation given to one or one hundred (or more) people.

How Will You Be Rewarded?
....

If you do not like the course you are currently on, you have to change it. When you decide to move forward with your goals to improve your performance, your life will change. When you adopt these principles, you will be able to create organized, colorful, and memorable presentations filled with anecdotes and humor. You will be able to implement many of the sales and closing techniques that you have "learned" but have never quite gotten to work. More important, you will have an improved level of success selling your ideas or your company's products. (I have seen many people who have completed my seminars wind up having significantly improved career opportunities.) You will be more motivated because you will feel as though you have control over the results of your efforts. In a sales presentation there are some things you can't change, but there are many things you can—if you learn how. Your arguments will be convincing, you will have better stories and anecdotes, and, most important, you will be having more fun.

Passion Is Everything

If there is one thing that makes a great presentation it is passion—the heartfelt emotion that says to your listener, "I truly believe in what I am saying." This is the single most convincing tool you have at your disposal. Build on your enthusiasm. This emotion is contagious, and people who know how to communicate it are able to light fires under the rest of humankind.

The skills necessary to communicate passion and enthusiasm can be learned. The catch is, you have to feel it. Dale Carnegie once said, "Act enthusiastic, and you will feel enthusiastic." That may be so, but you also have to be true to yourself. You must believe in three things in order to be able to express enthusiasm with conviction: You must believe in your product, you must believe in your company, and you must believe in yourself. If one of those three things is missing, make a change and fix it. Get off the fence. Find out what it will take for you to become a believer in those three parts of yourself, then do as Dale Carnegie said: Act enthusiastic. Later on, I will give you the techniques and exercises that will charge those listening to your presentation with the same explosive enthusiasm you feel about your topic.

To be great, a presentation has to be unique. No one is going to get very excited if you sound as though you got your pitch out of a Chinese fortune cookie. A man working as a telephone solicitor once told me that a woman on the line asked him point-blank if he was a recording. Can you imagine how little enthusiasm he must have possessed to be asked if his voice was a recorded message?

People sometimes ask me what the difference is between someone who sells a lot and someone who just barely gets by when both individuals appear similar and competent. I respond that it is usually a person's ability to analyze the audience and match a delivery style with listeners' preferences. In order to have a persuasive presentation, you will need to have done your homework on your audience. You must be able to give them a presentation that is customized to their needs, beliefs, and style. This takes preparation and requires doing the work necessary to find out something about your audience beforehand. Unfortunately, this isn't always possible. When it isn't, you have to use your "standard" presentation that you have found through experience to work most often on the majority of listeners.

A powerful sales presentation, by definition, is persuasive. If you haven't tried to make it persuasive, it probably isn't powerful. The techniques in this book will allow you to infuse your sales presentations with just the right degree of persuasiveness.

What Doesn't Contribute To A Great Presentation?

When I put people in front of a video camera during my training sessions, the first reaction they often have after seeing the playback is one of shock.

"Terri, I didn't realize how boring I sound!"

Yes, and sadly they are—boring. Why? Typically because they have never listened to themselves speak while imagining what it would be like to sit in the audience. Would you like to listen to you? Would you be persuaded by you? Would you buy from you? Another reason they aren't interesting is because, often, they think it doesn't matter if they are boring or not. Some people assume that, because they work for a large company, the firm's name alone will sell the product. Some people believe—erroneously—they are present only to deliver brochures and answer questions. To be effective they must do much more; they must be entertaining and worth listening to. Never let a great product or a great company get in the way of a great presentation.

The number one problem we find in working with sales professionals, however, is that their presentations rely on information rather than persuasion. Still influenced by the mindset of the affluent 1980s, salespeople tend to think if they give the client enough information, the sale will just fall in their laps. All presentations, however, have to be closed. If you don't get the order, you have wasted your time. If all you do is give out information, you are not likely to get a commitment from your prospect.

▼

The number one problem we find in working with sales professionals, however, is that their presentations rely on information rather than persuasion.

▲

By allowing your presentation to sound canned or appearing to just "go through the motions" you are simply sending yourself into another line of work. You have already quit, you just don't know it yet. I can guarantee you, however, that your audience knows it.

Can You Learn To Be Believable?

People buy people. If you sound convincing and enthusiastic, people will know that you are sold on your own product, and they will believe in it because they will believe in you. You can have all the selling tools at your disposal, the most marvelous product that engineers have ever designed, and the impeccable reputation of a company that has been in business for decades. But what counts is how clients perceive you and what you are saying. Are you believable or not? If you are, they likely will buy from you. If you are not, they will buy from your competitor, sometimes even when your competition offers an inferior product.

You can learn to communicate sincerity, a task which many people find difficult. This is not a book for slick operators who want to fool the public. This is a book for people who are sincere about what they are selling but could do a better job of getting their message across. We focus on those areas which you can control. We focus on your timing and organization. We build experience. We practice developing your skills during drills at home, before the actual presentation. You can learn to communicate more effectively.

▼

This is not a book for slick operators who want to fool the public.

▲

Know Your Audience

It is very easy to develop a single presentation and deliver it day in and day out to all kinds of people. The individual who does so is playing a numbers game. There is something to be said for playing the numbers, but results from such an approach have distinguishing characteristics often associated with random action: they are unpredictable and can promote burnout.

My intent is for you to stop wasting energy, refine your presentation, and focus your efforts in a way that will produce the best results possible for a given prospect. It helps to know your audience. Is it a group of teachers from Dubuque, or a team of biologists from the Department of Agriculture whose specialty is crop tolerance of salinity levels in river water? You have to know. In short, you have to do your homework. We will discuss audience more thoroughly in Chapter Five, "Tools of the Trade." It's important to understand, however, that to give a great presentation requires making the extra effort necessary to customize your talk and meet the needs of the individual or group who will hear it. It is an important part of making your presentation unique and memorable.

Accepting Change

The Lumberjack Story

Throughout your presentation you will want to use stories, anecdotes, and humor. Here is a little story my father told me, one that I use in my presentations to stress the importance of accepting new ideas.

Once upon a time there was a lumberjack who was known far and wide as the best in the forest. No matter who tried to beat him at chopping wood, no one could touch him. Every year the village where he lived sponsored a lumberjack festival in which people would compete in various events. The premier contest was wood chopping, and each year the old-timer would win hands down. Eventually, no one would challenge him. Other lumberjacks readily accepted the fact that this lumberjack could chop more wood in a day than anyone in the forest. He became the undisputed top producer.

One summer, however, a twenty-two-year-old apprentice lumberjack from outside the village came to the festival. Fresh out of lumberjack school, he was ambitious and wanted to make a name for himself, so he decided to challenge the old-timer. He figured that even if he lost, people would remember him. The old-timer agreed to the competition, and they decided the contest would last six hours. Both used the same type of ax so neither would have an advantage.

They went into the woods and had been chopping logs furiously for about two hours when suddenly the newcomer looked at his watch and declared, "You know, I think I'll take a break." The old-timer couldn't believe the challenger was tired so soon and just grinned as he shook his head, not missing a stroke with his ax. About twenty minutes later, the young man returned and continued his assault on his trees. They worked as fast as they could for another couple of hours. Suddenly, the challenger declared, "You know, I think I'll take another break." This statement caused the old-timer to scoff at the young man and mutter to himself that he should never have accepted the challenge. He was wasting his valuable time, he told the younger man, and he accused him of not being a serious contender. The young man finally returned after his break and the two finished the contest.

Everyone at the festival gathered around the huge piles of logs that the two lumberjacks had cut during the contest, and the count began to see which man had chopped the most wood. As the last log was counted, people stood confused and in a state of disbelief. The young lumberjack, even after taking two twenty-minute breaks, had more logs to his credit than the old-timer. Pandemonium broke out as the village realized it had a new champion. They handed him his trophy, and, as he started away, the old-timer came up and stopped him. "Hey, kid, hold on a minute. I've got to know what the heck it was you were doing when you were taking those twenty-minute breaks?"

The young man turned to the defeated champion and, maintaining an external sense of calm in his moment of triumph, said, "Well, friend, if you must know, I'll tell you. It's nothing more than everyone learns these days in lumberjack school. I used the time to sharpen my ax."

The moral of the story is simply that no matter how long you have been in any industry you can always find new ways to improve your performance. It never hurts to sharpen your tools! Keeping your tools razor sharp is what will keep you motivated, aggressive, and setting new goals.

Keeping Up With Change

Whether or not we accept it, times change, economies change, and businesses change. Whether or not we like it, if we fail to keep up with those changes we slide backward. The marketplace today is very different from that of the 1980s, and the sales professional needs different strategies to compete successfully. Salespeople need polished, believable, and highly persuasive presentations if they expect clients in the 1990s to give them their business.

Such presentations are a component of the evolution of sales and are marked by the increased level of sophistication we find in marketing in general that includes computer-generated graphics and sophisticated audiovisual presentations. The sales professional cannot sit on the sidelines and be overshadowed by the media he is using to display his products. He must be the leader and focus of attention in any presentation.

With honesty and integrity having become standards for the sales professional in the 1990s, the requirement to create a need in the mind of the prospect has become ever more important. The sales professional needs new tools to help him or her become more persuasive. As consumers become increasingly reluctant during a recession to part with their money, salespeople need to create what we call "harms."

We will talk more about these techniques of persuasion in a later chapter, but creating a harm means pointing out what undesirable consequence is apt to happen if the prospect does not buy your product or service. A harm has to be nonthreatening to avoid being manipulative; it has to be factual to conform to the standards of integrity that have been established. In selling in the 1990s, however, it will become a way to spur the client to action.

Information Overload

The proliferation of computers during the 1980s played a big role in dramatically increasing the amount of information available to buyers. Salespeople saw it as their sole responsibility to disseminate as much information as possible. It almost seemed as though it were part of a larger public relations campaign by their companies. Buyers wanted nothing more than to be informed and were quite capable, thank you, of making sound decisions on their own, based on the facts.

I suppose that scenario may have been all right when there was a strong enough market, but that is no longer the case in many industries. Salespeople are having to compete harder for the same business. This means that now, when they have a prospective client, they cannot afford to lose the sale. The sales-person needs to do everything within his or her control to complete the transaction.

Major Elements Of A Sale

Before we move into the specific techniques of persuasive pre-sentations, let's establish the basic four elements that constitute a sale. They are:

1. Attracting the prospect
2. Interesting the prospect
3. Convincing the prospect
4. Closing the sale

The progression of these elements is crucial. The important thing to remember is there are four distinct phases and each requires the prospect to undergo a change. If all we do is provide information, we fail to guide the client through the changes necessary to get from one phase to the next.

Chapter 2

SALESpeak

New Market Realities

Whether because of the Vietnam War, Watergate, or sobering competition from abroad, American business is under pressure today to give customers rock-solid value. For the sales professional, this means two things: He or she is going to have to present better arguments today for the superiority of his or her products and services, and he or she is going to have to relinquish the ancient crutch of manipulation. As consumers have become more sophisticated, the traditional hard close seems crude and unappealing. There is a dramatic shift today in consumer preferences away from manipulation and toward credibility.

Deception for years has served the useful purpose of helping to neutralize psychological restraints, allowing buyers to acquire what they want without guilt. People want to be sold. That principle still is true today. However, there is greater accountability now, both personally and in business, than there was several years ago regarding how people spend money.

With the accumulated debts and resultant interest payments left over from the 1980s and the lingering recession of the early 1990s, there simply isn't as much money to spend on discretionary items. People can't afford to make a purchasing error. They want all the facts up front. They want the best value for their money. They demand persuasive arguments.

In response, salespeople need to build their closing arguments as attorneys do. They need to show why a client should work with them and their company, and why they should do it now.

Salespeople Are Made, Not Born

The best salespeople always have had terrific skills of persuasion. It is not true these individuals had some God-given gift that others did not possess. Salespeople are made, not born. The sayings "he could sell ice cubes to Eskimos," or "he could talk the birds out of the trees" are used to describe the accomplishments of the most gifted salespeople. Sales training evolved from studying the habits and practices of these individuals who, by themselves, acquired the highly effective persuasive skills needed to convince people to buy. *Selling From A to Z*, the book by Tommy Hopkins, condenses the accumulated knowledge we have about sales. Anyone who reads that book, and others like it, or studies Hopkins's mentor, J. Douglas Edwards, can learn in a few hours what would take years to acquire through trial and error.

▼

The sayings "he could sell ice cubes to Eskimos," or "he could talk the birds out of the trees" are used to describe the accomplishments of the most gifted salespeople.

▲

As today's market grows leaner and more competitive, it also is becoming increasingly sophisticated. The basic techniques that allowed many salespeople to prosper during a period of easy credit and volume purchases may not be adequate for their success in the 1990s. Successful sales professionals now will be those who refine their skills of persuasion until they can present arguments so convincingly that an unwelcome hard close will be unnecessary.

The Evolution Of Selling

Traditional Pyramid
....

Let's look at the evolution of a sales presentation in more depth as we lead up to the best sales approach in today's marketplace. The traditional sales transaction may be described as a pyramid. Segments of increasing size represent the relative emphasis the salesperson places on each successive phase of the sales call. The introduction represents about 10 percent. It includes developing rapport with the client, establishing credibility, and creating common ground.

About 20 percent of the sales call consists of a needs analysis. What I refer to as the "DSM Theory" calls for the salesperson to D-etermine the client's needs, establish whether he or she can S-atisfy them, and arrive at how the salesperson can M-eet them.

The presentation accounts for 30 percent of the sales call. It includes the amount of information about the product or service the salesperson provides the client as well as organization and delivery.

In early sales models, the close represented the most significant element of the sales call. It accounted for 40 percent of the salesperson's success (see figure 1). The close might be any one of many. (Have you ever been to a seminar promising "160 surefire closes"?) Common ones include the "doorknob" close we mentioned earlier, or the "Ben Franklin" close, in which the benefits are listed against the drawbacks. Here the salesperson helps most on benefits, leaving the prospect to dream up drawbacks. Or it could be the "alternative" close, in which the client is presented not with a yes/no option, but with a choice such as, "Is Tuesday better for you, or Wednesday?" "Would green be prettier, or do you prefer red?"

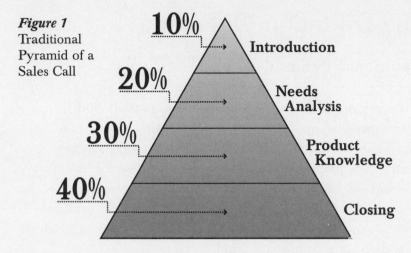

Figure 1
Traditional Pyramid of a Sales Call

10% ....⇢ **Introduction**

20% ....⇢ **Needs Analysis**

30% ....⇢ **Product Knowledge**

40% ....⇢ **Closing**

Refined Sales Techniques

Many sales trainers challenged the traditional pyramid in the 1980s. The result was the introduction of the "inverted pyramid." The new model reduced its emphasis on the close, an idea naturally heralded by sales professionals. "Now we don't have to close!" they cheered. Well, not quite, but the inverted pyramid does reflect a changing tone in selling.

These ideas developed partly from the knowledge that people make split-second decisions about whether they like you, often before you finish your presentation. Sometimes before you even start it! Trainers and theorists now allocated 40 percent of a sales call's success to the introduction. They elevated the needs analysis to 30 percent, while relegating product knowledge and presentation to 20 percent. The close, traditionally considered half the sale, suddenly was downgraded to 10 percent. People tried this new approach, and it worked. By building a good relationship with the client during the introduction, a salesperson could dif-

ferentiate herself from the crowd. Neither the traditional sales
model nor the inverted pyramid, however, took into account the
level of communication skills the salesperson had to rely upon in
formulating her presentation (see figure 2).

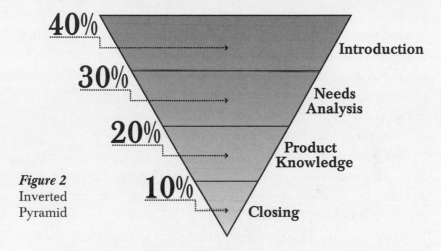

Figure 2
Inverted
Pyramid

A colleague shared with me the following story that truly
exemplifies the importance of communication skills in closing a
sale. When planners were expanding the John Wayne Airport in
Orange County, California, two major burger chains were com-
peting for a location within the airport. Although one company
thought it was a shoo-in because its headquarters were located in
Orange County, the franchise was awarded to its competitor.
Observers noted afterward that the winning company gave a
much more impressive presentation than the local firm that went
home in defeat. The winning concern presented airport officials
with an informative, entertaining—even humorous—presentation
that drove home, in point after point, the reasons they should be
awarded the contract. Was it any wonder the out-of-town group
won? Using advanced communication skills can give you a
tremendous advantage when persuading people to adopt your
point of view.

Little Things Mean A Lot

The "Three-To-Five-Company Rule"

··

When talking with a prospective client, you may safely assume yours is not the only game in town. For you to get to first base, the prospect must notice you and listen to what you have to say. For you to reach home plate, the client must perceive your product or service as outshining that of your competitor once the prospect has completed his value quest.

Yes, there is competition out there; you know it, and so do your prospects. They will exploit it because competition works to their advantage. The serious prospect will study between three and five companies before making a final selection. We call this the "Three-to-Five-Company Rule."

If yours is the first presentation heard, the prospect will resist making a buying decision until having had enough time to scout the market. If yours is the last presentation, the prospect will compare every detail of what you say against what he or she has been told by all the salespeople from other companies. In either case, your presentation will be critically evaluated. And so will you.

I always try to determine if my prospective clients are working with someone else. If I can't tell, I assume that they are. Doing so forces me to be even more persuasive and competitive than I would be otherwise.

Winning By A Nose

··

When facing competition, remember that your competitor's offer may be very similar, if not identical, to yours. Why then should the client buy from you? If you have ever been to the horse races, you know how close the winning horse can be to that in second place. The difference is sometimes "a nose." The difference in winnings, however, can be substantial, amounting to hundreds of thousands of dollars. The same thing is true in many competitive sports. Skiers in the 1994 Winter Olympics won gold medals on the basis of a few hundredths of a second—a small difference in performance, but a big difference in prizes.

The "80-20 Rule"

Ironically, leaders who win by a nose, or win by a couple of hundredths of a second, usually are not one-time winners. They do it time and again. We call this the "80-20 Rule." The 80-20 Rule is an application of the findings of Italian economist Vilfredo Pareto. He found that 20 percent of a society produced 80 percent of its income. In sales, 20 percent of the salespeople write 80 percent of the business. Training and development managers searched at length to learn what the top 20 percent do that the bottom 80 percent should be doing. The products are the same, the presentations are similar, the customers are from the same group. So how do they do it?

People Buy People

The Basic Walk

People say to me, "Terri, I can 'walk the walk,' but how do I 'talk the talk'?" I always see that question as a sign that someone is on the right track to becoming part of the top 20 percent. This individual realizes that the difference between being highly successful and merely average lies in his or her own actions and not with the product or company represented.

Let me give you an example from the real estate industry. It illustrates the considerable weight a salesperson has in influencing a prospect's selection. Suppose you want to sell your house. Employing the "Three-to-Five-Company Rule," you call several brokers to see who should get the listing. You choose Warmwell Banker, Millennium 21, and Provincial. All are nationwide companies with referral services. Brokers from each visit your house and describe their services to obtain your listing. Each asks for a 6 percent commission. All offer to list your home in the Multiple Listing Service. An agent who sold your neighbor's house brought all the salespeople and brokers from his office through the house on a "caravan." Naturally, you want the same thing. All three brokers assure you they will provide you with the identical service. Will they keep your house open Saturdays and Sundays, you ask? No problem.

▼

Top sales professionals give memorable presentations. They know not only how to walk the walk, they know how to talk the talk.

▲

The third broker leaves after finishing his presentation. You sit down and begin to figure out which company has the best program. What are the differences? You realize after struggling with the question, there are no differences! Each is identical. Each agent knew how to walk the walk and presented the features and benefits his company offers. There is one small difference, however. Each offer was made by a different person. So what are you going to do? Typically, you are going to pick the person you like the best. This happens over and over every day of the year. People pick the product based on who is selling it. People buy people. (If you haven't already done so, be sure to read Dale Carnegie's classic work, *How to Win Friends and Influence People,* that first addressed this topic.)

Now you say, "Well, Terri, I am what I am, and I can't change that. Either people like me or they don't." I am not advocating that you try to be someone you are not. You should always be true to yourself. People are going to like you based on what you say and do. In your role as a salesperson, that evaluation will be made based on your presentation. Do you want that presentation to sound lifeless, hesitant, and boring? Or do you want that presentation to sound enthusiastic, passionate, organized, and persuasive? When you are giving it, your presentation is you. It may be the only part of you that a prospect remembers—or forgets. Top sales professionals give memorable presentations. They know not only how to walk the walk, they know how to talk the talk.

The Three-Factor Difference

In my opinion, there are three major characteristics that typify top sales professionals. All believe they can be top producers, all have great persuasive presentation skills, and all are expert listeners. If I were to list a fourth characteristic it would be a good sense of timing, the ability to be in the right place at the right time to spot opportunities. However, I also believe there is no such thing as luck. As the old saying goes, "luck is when preparedness meets opportunity."

Dr. Denis Waitley in his audiotape series, *The Psychology of Winning*, discusses the psychological edge winners have in "believing" they can reach the ambitious goals they set for themselves. They "know" they can do it, so they try harder. If you think you can't do something, why waste your time even trying? Most people just compromise themselves by trying halfheartedly. That way, when they fail, they have an excuse for their poor performance. Besides, trying harder translates into more work. Fact: People who are lazy rarely make it to the top. Successful people do the things unsuccessful people don't want to do.

Dare To Dream

I am reminded of the movie, *Rudy*, about the life of Rudy Ruettiger, the Notre Dame football player who spent his entire college career preparing for a single game. His final moment of glory serves as testament to the fact that Rudy fulfilled his boyhood dream. Although Rudy had few innate talents when it came to football—a fact of which he was reminded during grueling practice sessions—his heart and soul cried out to be among the famous Fighting Irish. Rudy may have played only one game, but he never quit the team, nor was he cut. Many young men who get discouraged when they don't see enough action simply give up, but not Rudy. Today he can truthfully say that he played football for Notre Dame.

Rudy is now a successful motivational speaker whom I have had the pleasure of meeting. For years Rudy wanted to make a movie about his kooky football record because he thought it would be inspirational to others. The response from Hollywood: "You must be kidding!" Once again he didn't give up but kept knocking on doors until one finally opened. Eventually, his dream of producing a movie came true. The best part is the film received great reviews. Rudy Ruettiger's life is a success because he was willing to do what most other people will not do: Keep going when everyone else says, "Give up, it's hopeless—you're dreaming!" Remember never to let other people's limitations on you serve in place of your own goals.

There may be things about yourself you cannot change, but you do have control over several things that can take you from being among the average 80 percent to being in the top 20 percent. With practice you can improve your persuasive abilities and heighten your listening skills. These are two of the three critical elements in the Three-Factor Difference. Let me explain why focusing on these two skills can have such a dramatic influence on your earnings potential.

Sales Model For The 1990s

....

When salespeople adopted the inverted pyramid model that de-emphasized the close, many became "information providers." It was a way to establish themselves as professionals and avoid the negative reputation of the generation of hard closers that preceded them. The technique worked in the 1980s because the market was strong. The 1990s are leaner, and buyers are now good at evaluating products based on all the information we have been giving them. Importantly, buyers are making decisions faster than they were ten years ago. People expect all the pertinent information right from the starting gate.

Today's market demands a new model. I would like to offer one that I believe meets the needs of the sales professional in the 1990s. I call it the "Inverted Pyramid Circle." It is the inverted pyramid with a large circle around it. The circle represents the communication skills necessary for the model to work in a competitive environment. The model calls for a sales presentation based on highly polished public speaking skills. It has a logical, formulated argument with smooth transitions; and it employs stories, anecdotes, and humor to make it memorable. There is no hard sell, and the introduction continues to represent 40 percent of the task of completing the sale.

The Inverted Pyramid Circle depicts how all elements of the sales call depend upon the salesperson's skill to communicate well with the prospect. There is no attempt to quantify the importance of this skill because it affects the entire presentation. The model provides a new sales presentation element that will dramatically improve results of sales activities in the 1990s.

The Inverted Pyramid Circle emphasizes the need to create a logical, yet memorable, presentation. The model stresses the heightened importance the sales professional's personality plays in effecting the sale. Yet it suggests this attribute is merely a series of skills that can be separated into elements anyone can learn. Let me emphasize that I am not saying someone can learn to have a personality. Each of us already has a personality, but we can learn how to express it better (see figure 3).

Figure 3
Inverted
Pyramid
Circle

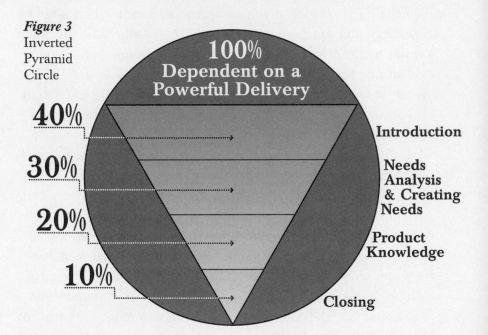

100%
Dependent on a
Powerful Delivery

40% ⟶ Introduction

30% ⟶ Needs
Analysis
& Creating
Needs

20% ⟶ Product
Knowledge

10% ⟶ Closing

The Future of Presentations

Technology And The New Sales Professional

At the same time we are discussing ways of giving a presentation greater personal appeal with more enthusiasm, someone is working in a computerized editing room putting the finishing touches on a dynamic sight-and-sound show, more colorful and impressive than any we have ever seen. As far as presentations go, this is the wave of the future.

There are two things to remember about the use of audiovisuals. The first is that you should never relinquish your leadership position to a videotape. The live speaker is the star of any show and should not abdicate that title. All the audiovisual tools at his disposal are just that–tools. The second thing is that it demands more from the speaker to retain his leadership position with an audience as these tools become more sophisticated. The speaker must have a good delivery style.

▼

The live speaker is the star of any show and should not abdicate that title.

▲

The challenge for the future is how to use these new technologies while retaining the presentation's human element. A videotape may be impressive, but it takes a sales professional to communicate the message and to be persuasive.

Chapter 3

Listening Communication Skills

We Don't Listen, But Why?

A Matter Of Perspective

There is a joke about a famous psychiatrist who is approached at a cocktail party by a solicitous guest. "My dear doctor," he begins. "How can you stand to listen to people's problems all day long? It must be dreadfully depressing." Somewhat taken aback by the man's provocative question, but determined not to be easily annoyed, the psychiatrist quips: "Listen? Who listens?"

I have many clients who come to my training programs because they are concerned about their speaking skills. They realize if they can improve their presentations they will be more effective sales professionals. Almost no one, however, worries about their listening skills—at least not until they see themselves on videotape and realize they need help. You may have heard the quotation from writer Ambrose Bierce, who once said, "A bore is a person who talks when you wish him to listen...." Listening is an active process that requires intense thought. We need to listen to our clients and prospects as well as to ourselves.

We Just Don't Get It

When we tape participants in a sales training role-play session, they often say, "Now I understand what the customer's question was!" The comment usually comes after they realize they didn't answer the prospect's question, or they responded with an answer that would send any rational person across the street into the waiting arms of the competition. Often we don't hear what our clients are saying, or we select an answer that is inappropriate because we really don't understand the question. Our mouths take charge after our brain shuts down. We just don't take the time to listen. If we slip into autopilot and respond mechanically, I guarantee it does not impress our audience.

The Listening Investment

The irony in our absentee attention span is, while we may not listen very well, we spend lots of time doing it. As sales professionals, we expend nearly three-fourths of our working time communicating, and 42 percent of *that* in listening. The rest we divide between speaking, reading, and writing, with speaking representing a third of our efforts. Reading represents about 15 percent and writing 11 percent. When a third of our entire working time is spent listening to others, doesn't it make sense we should examine our listening habits even before we polish our speaking skills?

Can We Influence Retention?

Good Listeners Are Rare

Ronald R. Allen and Ray C. McKerrow in their book, *Pragmatics of Public Communication*, suggest the reason we pay little attention to developing our listening skills is that we take them for granted. To become better listeners we need to understand what listening is and to take a fresh look at this undervalued, but extremely important, sales activity.

Surely you can think of someone who is a particularly impressive listener. He or she remembers things we tell them, asks insightful questions, and generally makes us feel good by leaving us with the impression of truly understanding—and therefore caring about—what we say. Unfortunately, most of the time we don't live up to that standard—nor do our clients. One of the reasons people don't listen and retain information is that they are bored. We have to sell people on listening to us in order to maintain their attention. Every college student knows the professor who comes to class and reads the same flat lecture, from the same boring notes, in the same monotone voice, every semester. The result is students falling asleep. We must be interesting and entertaining if we want people to listen.

"Let Me Sleep On It"

On average, prospects will retain only half of what we tell them. Before an hour has passed, they lose 10 percent of the little they originally knew. After going home and sleeping on it, guess what? Another 20 percent has evaporated overnight. And they started with only 50 percent in the first place! By the time the breakfast rush has subsided, they have avoided two near-collisions on the freeway, found notes on their desks from their bosses, and have forgotten another 10 percent. So the entire time we have assumed a prospect has been thinking about our proposal, he or she has been literally *forgetting* about it.

Understanding—Key To Remembering

We can help improve our clients' retention by creating a presentation worth listening to and by improving our own listening skills. We can help our prospects remember our presentation by influencing whether they understand it in the first place—a big factor in how much of it they remember. Improving our listening skills also will help us overcome our prospects' objections and even give us better control over the sales situation.

Listening And Control

Imagine a situation in which the prospect is trying to wrest control of the sales call. Imagine yourself trying to maintain control to close the sale. Now think of yourself engaged in these activities: focusing the conversation on the points you want to make, listening to the client's comments, responding to them, presenting your argument, listening, responding, presenting.

To some extent, every prospect is difficult, and every transaction requires expert listening skills to connect with the client and close the sale.

Now imagine yourself in a similar situation with a difficult prospect, only instead of engaging the person, you are ignoring what they are saying, choosing instead to recite the list of features and benefits of your product. This is a situation more common than you might imagine; through videotape playback and workshop drills, we find that people frequently "tune out" their prospects' questions and also their objections.

In which of these two situations are you going to have the greatest chance for success? The first one, of course, because you are exercising control over the sale and continuing to guide the prospect toward the close. To some extent, every prospect is difficult, and every transaction requires expert listening skills to connect with the client and close the sale.

The Dimensions Of Listening

Empathic Listening

There are three dimensions to listening that account for how well we hear what the prospect says. The first is empathy and means that we listen from the heart. We avoid prejudging the prospect's statements. Have you heard the phrase, "buyers are liars"? It is a cynical comment you will want to ignore. The buyer may well employ counterfeit objections but also will have legitimate concerns. Your job is to decipher which of his or her stated concerns are bogus and which are real. To discount all the prospect's objections without determining the facts is to act without empathy. Listen for the buyer's true concerns. Be empathic.

Information Processing

The second dimension of listening is information processing. It means objectively collecting and categorizing facts from the prospect, then prioritizing what you hear. There are separate activities associated with information processing. To be an information processor, you must:

1. Recognize the central idea
2. Identify main points
3. Recall details
4. Summarize
5. Draw references
6. Ask insightful questions

In my workshops, I usually ask salespeople, "What is the goal of your presentation?" They look at me as though they don't know what I'm talking about. "What do you mean?" they ask. Well, what is the point of your presentation? Do you really know what the single, overriding message is that you are trying to get across? If you aren't clear on what your central idea is, your prospective client isn't going to know either. You may have been working in your field for twenty years, you may have all the supporting figures in your head to prove a long string of claims, but if you can't tell your message in a way that makes people understand the main points, you will be spinning your wheels.

If your clients cannot recognize the central idea of your message, if they cannot identify the main points, recall important details, summarize the information, and ask insightful questions, then you have to wonder, "How effective was I?" Try putting yourself in the role of one of your clients and see if you can apply the above criteria to your presentation. Then try it on feedback from your next customer. Be aware of yourself as a deliverer of information.

Critical Listening

A listener will critically evaluate your presentation, including every claim in it, whether you pay attention to what you are saying or whether you put your mouth on automatic and flip the "on"

▼

Remember, the customer is testing your credibility.

▲

switch. What happens, though, when your prospect asks a question? Are you going to respond in a way that reinforces your message and continues moving him or her toward the close? Or are you going to confuse the prospect with a response that isn't really related to the question asked? Remember, the customer is testing your credibility. Are both you and what you say believable? In order to use the excellent opportunity a question offers, you will need to develop and employ critical listening skills. Remember that your prospects will be listening to you from a critical standpoint as well.

If you heard your own presentation and you wanted to evaluate it for credibility, how would you do it? Here are the five keys to assessing the third listening dimension, critical listening:

1. Recall main claims
2. Identify the premise
3. Evaluate evidence
4. Be objective, not defensive
5. Ask how credible is the speaker

Since your listeners will critically evaluate your presentation by performing these steps, doesn't it make sense for you to do the same evaluation of your presentation before delivering it? After all, if your talk is so muddled you have trouble evaluating it, how can you expect your prospect to be influenced positively by it?

Listening To Questions

In practice, many of your prospects will not be good critical listeners. They will jump to conclusions based on personal experiences that may have little or nothing to do with what you have been telling them. If you are a good critical listener, you can recognize these misinterpretations when the prospect poses a question. You will be applying your critical listening skills to the feedback you get.

The important thing is for your prospect to hear the right message and not make a decision based on incorrect assumptions. It is crucial, therefore, to be objective in evaluating your client's questions and comments. You can clarify and reinforce your points on the way to guiding the prospect toward the close.

SALESpeak

Chapter 4

Persuasive Speaking:
The Career Enhancer

The benefits of knowing how to speak effectively in public with a logical, formulated presentation can be highly rewarding. As a sales professional, you spend much of your time giving presentations to individuals. On occasion, you probably deliver talks to larger audiences. Knowing how to do so effectively can give a major boost to your career and expand your sphere of influence in your territory and/or industry. Many of the skills needed to speak before a large audience are the same ones that improve one-on-one presentations.

Never Underestimate The Power Of Your Presentation

A client of mine was asked to speak at a public meeting in support of a local political candidate. Citizens were attempting to rout incumbents from an elected board, and the new office seeker provided fresh ideas. My client accepted the public speaking challenge because he felt it was the right thing to do. Besides, his wife already had accepted the invitation on his behalf. For the purpose of this story, I will call my client Bob.

Plea For Help

....

When he called me, Bob was terrified at the prospect of addressing a large audience. He had little experience and less self-confidence. I got his desperate plea on a Friday.

"Terri, I don't know what I'm going to do," he said. "I have to make a presentation in front of six hundred people at a political rally next week. Can you help me?"

I said, "Sure, Bob. No problem." After all, he was the one who would have to give the speech—all I had to do was to coach him! We began work on his talk by creating an outline. We established the main points he would make, developed the supporting material, and put in the stories and anecdotes. We worked on the talk all weekend. By the meeting Monday night, Bob was about as ready as he was going to be. If you have ever been to a heated public gathering, you can appreciate how intimidating it can get. This was no office staff meeting where people are paid to sit quietly and pay attention. This was an emotion-packed gathering of concerned citizens.

Whew, It's Over—Or Is It?

....

Bob walked into the large auditorium and strolled to the podium. His knees were shaking, but the average person couldn't tell he was scared. No matter how nervous he was, we both knew he could do it. As he began his talk, it became clear his speech had a framework. It was logical, it adhered to the proper formula, and it had a specific objective he wanted to fulfill. It had impact, it was memorable—and it worked. The audience rose to their feet, clapped, cheered, and whistled. He was a star with a smash hit. His first thought, however, was not what a great job he had done. It was, "Whew, it's over!" Except it wasn't over. There was someone in the audience Bob hadn't noticed. Bob's vice-president, three management levels above him, was among the attendees.

New Position Opens

"Bob, I had absolutely no idea," the executive began. "You are a powerful speaker. I want to talk to you about a position we have coming up that requires someone with your skills. If you are free tomorrow about nine o'clock, stop by my office so we can discuss it."

Not only did Bob do well during the interview, suddenly he found himself within the executive inner circle. With his new position, he received a substantial raise, bonus structure, and car allowance. That isn't bad for a free talk. The story has a happy ending, but what if Bob had declined the speaking engagement? He would have missed a great opportunity for self-improvement. As it was, Bob's sphere of influence and his position, not to mention his income, were enhanced. Though Bob was extremely anxious about the task, he tried it anyway—and succeeded!

▼

You may think you are talking to someone of limited means and authority. However, "little fish" have a habit of traveling with "big fish."

▲

Had Bob "winged" his talk, as many people do, it would not have had the same impact. With a lackluster performance, he probably wouldn't have been approached about the job opening. It is important to put passion into every presentation and to do adequate advance planning in order to create opportunities. You may think you are talking to someone of limited means and authority. However, "little fish" have a habit of traveling with "big fish."

Short Talks Count

When you give a talk, never underestimate the power of your pitch. That holds true even for a seemingly insignificant presentation. It is possible to have an impact in mere seconds. I recently attended a conference sponsored by the Harvard Business School alumni. There primarily to network, I tried to figure out a discreet way of promoting my public speaking and training services to as many attendees as possible.

During the question/answer session, I stood up and asked the panel members what they thought were the three most significant characteristics of a good chief executive officer. Naturally, in the course of my brief self-introduction, I had identified myself, my company, and the types of services my company offers. Giving them this information was a start, but to connect with someone, I knew I would have to provide a direct call to action. I then mentioned that I happened to be looking for a CEO to run my own company. I invited anyone who felt he or she possessed these characteristics and was interested in a career change to speak to me during the break.

Initially the remark sent the audience into laughter. I knew that I had entertained them and, in the process, made them remember me. Even better, about half a dozen people introduced themselves to me afterward. I didn't wind up hiring any of them, but, as it turned out, two of them later hired me to speak to their organizations. My thirty-second talk turned into speaking contracts worth thousands of dollars.

To reinforce the point that the length of a presentation doesn't necessarily indicate its relative importance, I recall a wedding I attended where the best man rose to give the customary toast to the bride and groom. The aftermath was a chorus of regrets. "How pathetic," people said. "He could barely utter the words, he was so nervous." If the best man had done a better job preparing for his moment of glory, all he would have heard afterward was how insightful and clever he had been.

You have the opportunity as a professional to deliver sharp, inspiring, memorable presentations. Or you can deliver limp, lifeless talks that don't persuade anyone to do anything except, perhaps, promise to call you later. One type of presentation makes money, the other doesn't. The choice is up to you.

Understanding Persuasive Presentations

There are different ways to deliver information, but the one you need to master is that of persuasion. You say, "I'm not like that," or "I don't know how to do that, Terri. I don't have that kind of personality." It doesn't take a certain kind of personality, all it takes is having one—and everyone does. All you have to do is learn how to express it.

The Call To Action

The two main differences between a persuasive talk and either a ceremonial or informative talk are that the persuasive talk begins by building an argument and it concludes with a call to action (the close). A persuasive presentation is one that leads your client toward doing something specific. Usually that means signing the contract or setting up the next appointment.

Ceremonial Speeches

There are other types of presentations too, such as ceremonial and informative. Ceremonial speeches appeal to the values cherished by everyone present. The speaker tries to create a type of communion with the audience. Award ceremonies, acceptance, keynote, after-dinner, welcome, and farewell speeches all fall into this category.

Informative Talks

Informative speeches are the most common and the most common trap for salespeople. When they should be delivering a persuasive speech, they give an informative one instead. The informative speech should not be the salesperson's tool of choice, although you would never know it by how many people use it. Informative presentations are objective. They promote audience understanding, foster cooperation, and present the subject matter in an unbiased way. The whole point is to promote learning. As a salesperson, do you want to educate your customer, or do you want to sell him something? True, sometimes we want to do both, but too often we accomplish only one objective—the wrong one. If you find you are completing fewer sales than you would like, ask yourself if your presentation is informative or persuasive. Chances are it is too informative.

Just for practice, try repeating the following phrase out loud: "As a sales professional, I am not an informative presenter."

Right, as a sales professional, you are not an informative speaker. You are a persuasive speaker.

And now, try repeating this: "As a sales professional, I am a persuasive presenter."

Fine. Just keep repeating that to yourself.

The "Information Zone"

You may ask, "Well, Terri, shouldn't my presentation be both persuasive and informative?" Yes it should be, but speakers have a tendency to linger in the "information zone." Either they are not persuasive enough, or they save the persuasive material until the very end when it is too late. The customer has little incentive to make a buying decision following a predominantly informative presentation. There is no sense of urgency in an informative presentation.

One reason salespeople stay in the information zone is they never hear the word "no." The client may say, "Great, thanks for the information!" Meanwhile, you, or they, walk out the door. Of course you hope they will feel guilty enough later to give you the business. I have news for you. Customers who don't buy don't feel guilt. True, you won't hear the word "no" in the information zone. You won't hear the word "yes" either.

Communication Apprehension

People have varying levels of apprehension about giving persuasive talks, particularly when they arrive at the point where they call the listener to action. Communication apprehension is the fear or uneasy feeling we have as we anticipate the presentation we are about to deliver to an important client.

Try to determine where you are on this continuum by drawing a line on a sheet of paper. Label the left end "high apprehension" and the right "low apprehension." Draw an "X" on the line where you think your feelings would place you. The "X" indicates whether you see yourself as a low-apprehension or high-apprehension communicator (see figure 4).

Now draw a second line and label the left part "introduction" and the right part "close." Imagine this to be a sales call. Think of yourself beginning to speak with a client. You move through the introduction toward the close.

Figure 4

Level of Communication Apprehension

High ←————————————————→ Low

A Typical Sales Call

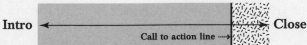

Intro ←————————————————→ Close

Call to action line ---→

The 80-20 Rule*

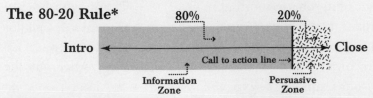

80%   20%

Intro ←————————————————→ Close

Call to action line ---→

Information Zone   Persuasive Zone

*Eighty percent of sales professionals tend to be informative vs persuasive. The top 20% of sales professionals tend to be persuasive vs informative.

What happens? You start to feel anxious when you near the close. Place an "X" at that point on your line. That is where most people move from the information portion to the "call for action." At the beginning of your talk you were in a low-apprehension region. As you moved toward the point where you would have to ask the prospect to do something, you entered a high-apprehension area. The beginning is informative, but the end is persuasive.

Draw a third line on the paper under first two. Intersect the line on the right side eight-tenths of the way over. Think of this as representing the 80-20 rule. Do you see a correlation between your comfort level with public speaking and your ability to close? Those who have a greater fear of public speaking tend to linger in the information zone. Those who have greater confidence in their speaking skills have greater "closing skills" comfort. Does your "X" correlate with your current sales production?

One approach that has been developed to manage this critical issue is to make your presentation persuasive right from the start.

Persuasive From Beginning To End

The type of presentation you will want to develop to avoid slipping into the information zone is persuasive throughout, not just at the end. Although the latter is more common, it is better to be persuasive throughout the entire presentation. For one thing, it puts less pressure on you as you approach the close—making the task easier. It also puts less pressure on your customer because you build your case throughout your talk as you lead him or her toward a decision.

The focus is on influencing the buyer's perceptions by carefully managing our supporting material. I will show you how to do this later. Meanwhile, keep in mind that our intent is to sell the listener our product, service, or idea. If that doesn't happen, our efforts to provide him or her with information have been at our own—or our employer's—expense.

Five Parts To A Persuasive Presentation

When we talk about influencing perception, we mean using language to influence a person's beliefs. Listeners have to relate your information to their individual situations and see themselves benefiting from what you have to offer. There are four foundation characteristics of a persuasive presentation. Such a presentation must:

1. Be interactive
2. Be convincing
3. Create a harm (a need)
4. Provide a choice
5. Be competitive

Being Interactive

There must be a give-and-take between the salesperson and the customer. There cannot be simply one-way communication. The interactive or "transactional" aspect of a persuasive talk is what scholars call the "Socratic approach." The speaker or salesperson must ask the right questions, listen to the answers, and respond before the presentation's conclusion. Try creating a presentation that answers common objections *before* a prospect can ask them. I call this approach "creating a proactive presentation." It is to be preferred over a reactive presentation, which merely informs the listeners and invites their objections, which then must be overcome.

▼

The interactive or "transactional" aspect of a persuasive talk is what scholars call the "Socratic approach."

▲

Being Convincing

To be convincing, the presentation has to be logical. You will find it very difficult to create a compelling presentation without developing your argument. The following is a five-step process used to arrive at a logical persuasive argument:

1. Generate awareness
2. State the problem
3. Provide a solution
4. Visualize change
5. Call for action

Generating Awareness

When I refer to generating awareness, I mean making the prospect aware of his or her needs. People approach a salesperson with different levels of awareness about what they really need or want. Sometimes too, customers have no understanding at all of the product or service. Depending on how much they know, we have to help them out. How many times have you ever worked with people who didn't know what they needed?

Stating The Problem

The reason most people buy products is because they have a need, or problem. The product, or service, solves—or relieves them of—their problem. Generally, the problem is defined in terms of time, money, or an emotional need.

Providing A Solution

The salesperson needs to show the prospective client how the product or service being sold provides a solution to the client's problem. Providing the solution is a necessary element of creating a convincing, logical argument. If you are going to make your clients aware of their problems, you owe it to them to relieve their stress. You do this by providing a solution—buying your product or service. Doing so should save them time, money, or possibly their sanity! Have you ever heard the objection, "Your product (service) costs too much"? The following story will provide you with a response that is effective in overcoming this type of objection.

I travel a lot and am usually in a rush when checking out of a hotel. It's not uncommon for me to leave something behind, and this time it was my running shoes—one running shoe, to be specific. When I arrived home, I told my mother I needed to buy another pair, and she suggested I go to the local warehouse discount store where she holds a membership.

I had never shopped at one of these outlets before and wasn't expecting to have to park a half mile away. Nevertheless, I made the hike to the entrance, where I was stopped by an employee who asked to see my membership card. So I began fishing through my purse for our card. People began piling up behind me, then pushed me out of the way to get inside. Finally I produced the card and was allowed to enter.

Since there is no shoe department, I wandered around looking for someone to ask where they keep the running shoes. Well, there were no clerks either, at least I couldn't find anyone. Finally I saw a big stack of shoes. Since they weren't in any order, I had to paw through the entire bin just to find my size. Great! Size seven—I was in luck. I opened the box, and inside—there was only one shoe. So I dug around some more and found another box of size sevens. I tucked it under my arm and headed toward the checkout counter. The checkout line must have had twenty-five people, and they all had huge carts full of merchandise. I stood in line for more than twenty minutes just to buy one pair of shoes. Then, when I got to the cashier, he wouldn't take my credit card. It turned out the store didn't accept most major cards. I finally made it back to my car and realized I had wasted nearly an hour to save less than ten dollars. Besides that, I was exhausted and in a terrible mood.

About a month later, I came home from another trip and, guess what? I had lost another shoe, one of the brand-new ones I had just bought. The thought of going back to the warehouse almost made me ill. I thought to myself, "This time, I'm going to Bullocks!" (one of the leading Southern California department store chains). I got in my car, drove over to the store, and there was a valet waiting. He opened the door, asked me how long I would be, and, smiling, took my car keys and presented me with a receipt. I proceeded right into the store with no hassle parking, no long trek from the lot—I just stepped right into the store. I walked straight to the shoe department where the clerk politely asked me what I was interested in wearing. I told him the brand, the size, and in less than a minute, I had a shoe on my foot. "Perfect," I said, and he asked me whether I would like to pay by cash or credit card. He took my credit card (I didn't even have to get out of my seat) and asked me if I wanted to take the shoes with me, or if I would like to have them shipped. Delighted, I asked him to ship them. He returned with my card, the charge, and shipping slips for me to sign, and I was out of there!

I tipped the valet a dollar, slipped behind the wheel, and I was back on the road. I had saved maybe forty minutes (that I could use putting together my next presentation) and I was in a great frame of mind. Was it worth the extra ten dollars? You bet! So any time someone says your product or service costs too much, simply show them how it saves them time or helps preserve their sanity, which is worth a lot more money in the long run.

Visualizing Change

As a sales professional, you must help prospects visualize change. You have to take them from their present "miserable" condition to that enhanced lifestyle you envision for them. Unless they can see themselves moving into a new dimension, they won't be convinced your product or service is necessary.

Taking Action

The final logical element in preparing a persuasive presentation is the call to action. This is the most important of the five steps. If you don't tell customers what you want them to do, they may misinterpret your message. They might not buy anything at all. They could even buy from someone else. You can't afford to take that chance. If you have developed the earlier part of your presentation in a convincing way, the customer already agrees with you. The call to action, therefore, sounds completely appropriate.

Creating "Harms"

Clients may realize they could use a product or service similar to yours but may not have sufficient motivation to buy it. If they do decide to buy, will they shop for other products returning to yours because it is best?

In the 1980s, salespeople got used to assuming consumers eventually would buy their products and services. It was just a question of which brand. The answer was to sell them on "features and benefits."

Selling with features and benefits, popular in the 1980s, is much more difficult today. In lean times, people tend to eliminate the "extras" because they think they can't afford them. They will purchase only what they feel they need. The salesperson must develop a sense of urgency in the mind of the client in order to stimulate a transaction. Unfortunately, there is no sense of urgency in a features-and-benefits presentation. A feature is what the product *is*. A benefit is what it *does*. For a prospect to understand why he or she must acquire our product or service, we must create a need or point out the "harm" likely to occur if they don't use what we have to offer. In the 1990s, a salesperson's job is to "create" needs, not just to do a needs analysis.

In order to act, clients must be convinced they can't get along without the product. To convince them, the salesperson today can create a "harm." What is a harm? It is a tool used by debaters, attorneys, and politicians that we, as sales and business professionals, can use to build our arguments and make our cases before our prospects or audience. A harm is that problem your customer or listener might encounter if they don't buy your product, service, or point of view.

While it may seem harsh, we face the prospect everyday of dealing with harms. Unfavorable situations are depicted through advertising on radio and television, in newspapers and magazines. The creation of harms in the media is a very clear adaptation to changes in economic conditions from the 1980s to the 1990s. The purpose is to *create* consumer needs.

In the 1980s, when selling was easier, and harms weren't necessary, a widely known mouthwash company promoted the features and benefits of their product. People were shown kissing in a variety of situations, and the message was: If you use this mouthwash, someone will want to—and most likely will—kiss you. The ad sold the product's features and benefits. The feature was its breath-freshening action, the benefit was the pleasurable experience of being kissed.

In today's market, stating the problem means creating a "harm." A commercial touting the same product is significantly different from that of the previous decade. It begins by creating a *need* for mouthwash. We see the husband waking up with "morning breath," a sickly fog floating from his mouth. He has to go to the bathroom and use mouthwash before receiving a kiss. What is the harm? Morning breath! Do you really want to see the eyes of your spouse fill with tears after you plant a kiss?

You avoid the harm by buying and using the product so you will have fresh breath. Buying the mouthwash no longer is a luxury. The viewer *needs* it in case he or she has morning breath. The advertisement still promotes the feature and benefit of kissing, but does so at the end.

Another TV ad that clearly depicts a harm is one promoting car phones. A woman becomes stranded at night in a bad part of town after her car breaks down. From inside the vehicle, she looks across the street to a lighted telephone booth and clearly is thinking about calling for help. The camera then zooms over to a group of thugs loitering around the phone booth. The viewer's first thought is, "This situation looks dangerous—don't get out of the car!" Her options are not appealing. The scene is then replayed with the car stalling. The woman glances at the phone booth, the thugs, but then she looks down at her car phone. The situation appears a lot more manageable. Needless to say, the ad is not only directed at women who drive, but also at the husbands and boyfriends of those women, who can easily see the potential danger. The ad makes a car phone no longer a luxury, but rather a necessity in case of an emergency.

Tire commercials are another example of the way advertisers create harms. The awful thing that could happen to you if you don't own a particular brand of tire is strongly suggested by an abrupt stop just before a major accident is about to occur.

Volvo, the automobile maker, creates a harm in the minds of TV viewers when it shows a mannequin being tossed around inside a crashing car. The harm is, if you are not in a Volvo and you get in an accident like this one, you could be crushed. Look for commercials with harms in them. They permeate today's media.

How To Create A Harm

To create a harm that will help sell your product or service in today's challenging marketplace, ask yourself what would happen to your clients if they didn't work with you and your company? What would happen if they didn't do it now?

Anyone can create a harm, no matter what the situation. The example I like to use in my seminars comes from the courtroom where our defendant, Mr. Smith, is on trial for murder. If you were the prosecutor, you would argue to the jury that it must convict Smith or he will be free to commit another horrible crime. The harm is that the population will be at risk if the jury releases Smith back to the streets.

If you were Smith's defense attorney, however, you would tell jurors that any murderer should be put behind bars. However, since Smith didn't do it, the jury will be convicting an innocent man. The real killer, meanwhile, will remain at large, free to murder again. The harm is that the jury will have committed a gross miscarriage of justice by imprisoning an innocent man, not to mention failing in its responsibility of fairly trying one of its peers.

No matter which side of the case you represent, you can create a harm to support your position. The same rules apply to a persuasive sales presentation. The whole point of creating harms is to build the sense of urgency in the client. Try to build the harm at the beginning of your presentation, then sell the features and benefits at the end.

Some people may want to use only one or two harms, while others will find the opportunity to build their entire presentation around a harm or series of harms. Remember, this is just one of many instruments you can use to make your presentation persuasive. In the following chapter, we will discuss additional tools you can employ in your efforts to persuade the client to take action.

Providing A Choice

By creating a harm, in effect we create a choice for the customer. Sometimes we have to be very specific in defining his or her options. The most frequently cited harm is the risk of working with someone other than ourselves—someone who easily could be unsatisfactory. Everyone has had poor service from a vendor. If customers don't work with you, they run the risk of working with someone less:

1. Efficient
2. Effective
3. Ethical
4. Timely
5. Friendly
6. Enthusiastic

One risk in creating choices for the prospect, particularly with a harm, is in overdoing it. We never want to denounce a competitor. Neither do we want to create an undue sense of duress in the prospect while creating our harm. Granted, there is a fine line. With practice, providing the customer with a choice that presents a harm becomes second nature.

Of course you would never use the term "harm" in a presentation itself. It is just a word to trigger the mindset of someone building a persuasive argument. I learned it from a debate coach who taught me how to build an effective case, and I have been unable to find another word that better describes this technique.

Being Competitive

The nature of a persuasive presentation means it tries to change people from believing in one set of ideas to having faith in another. It challenges the status quo by promoting a set of values not yet shared by the listener. It refutes existing ideas that may be held by the customers or audience. The talk allows the speaker to compete successfully for their allegiance.

Four Speech Formats

There are several ways in which people deliver persuasive presentations. Format is important because it affects how we prepare for our talks. There are advantages and disadvantages to each style. Here are the four presentation formats:

1. Impromptu
2. Extemporaneous
3. Manuscript
4. Memorized

Impromptu

An impromptu presentation is just that—no preparation. It is delivered without rehearsal. It provides great freedom to interact with the audience and, if done well, can show how knowledgeable you are about your subject. Yet giving an impromptu talk has distinct disadvantages when you are trying to be persuasive. Obviously, you don't have time to prepare or develop an argument. Recalling and selecting just the right words to describe what you are talking about also can be a challenge for many people when giving impromptu talks.

Extemporaneous

An extemporaneous presentation is one you prepare in advance and deliver from an outline. The presentation is not written word-for-word. The most common format for the sales professional, it allows the presenter to adjust his or her presentation as questions arise.

Drawbacks include the possibility of forgetting words necessary to nail down arguments precisely. If you have ever stumbled during a presentation while trying to find the right word, you understand the problem. The presentation can also become lopsided if the speaker spends too much time on the beginning and rushes through the second half to meet time constraints.

Manuscript

The speaker reads every word of a manuscript presentation. He or she knows that what will be said is exactly what is intended. The speaker knows the language will remain vivid and compelling and that the presentation will stay within fixed time limits.

Manuscripts are used to deliver important messages, say by a government spokesman or at a scientific seminar. Disadvantages include the likelihood the discourse will sound like an essay since people rarely write the way they speak. The talk may also sound stiff. The style makes it difficult to react spontaneously to the listener or audience. It requires a great deal of preparation to make it sound professional and not canned.

Memorized

A memorized presentation is written in manuscript form and committed to memory. This format was very popular in years past. Today, most salespeople prefer the extemporaneous presentation. I personally endorse the memorized format because it allows the salesperson to focus on his or her audience. It is particularly effective in formal presentations. However, it requires extensive practice and commitment in order to be employed effectively because, if your mind goes blank... need I say more?

Thorough Preparation

No matter which format you choose, remember to keep track of where you are headed with your argument. People ask me whether it really is necessary to do this much work before giving a talk. I know from experience even extremely talented people generally do not cover everything unless they list all the issues on paper first, then study them. When you "wing it," you tend to leave out important ideas or stray off course. People spend too much time on issues that don't deserve it, while more important points get underemphasized.

One effective exercise we do in our training sessions is to videotape sales professionals responding to objections they have written out and placed in a hat. When they realize these objections occur repeatedly, they see how much more persuasive they could be if only they practiced and memorized the responses ahead of time.

Having your presentation and answers to questions memorized in advance is useful, particularly since a prospective client may allow you only a few minutes. Even better is including the answers to your most commonly asked questions right in your presentation.

A lot of work goes into a good presentation. This is particularly true when you want to tailor your talk to each individual audience or prospect. In the next chapter, "Tools of the Trade," we will discuss how to customize your presentation for each new listener.

Chapter 5

Tools of the Trade

First Rule In Self-Improvement: Commitment

People admire a polished, professional presentation for several reasons. For one, they sense how much work goes into preparing it. For another, they are impressed with how such a presentation can effect change, which is always a challenging undertaking. They also respect the fact that one who prepares and practices is far above average because most people don't–they wing it.

The presentation our client or audience hears is the result of many hours of preparation. We might liken it to the tip of an iceberg. It may be short, but it carries the potential to breach the hull of a Titanic mindset.

There are several ways to prepare for a presentation. I call them the tools of the trade. All relate to the intense preparation necessary to give a really good talk. Remember that our goal should be to achieve excellence. To do that we must propel ourselves away from our familiar–but sometimes sloppy and ineffective–delivery style.

We must try for a compelling sales presentation that moves people to action. This requires making a commitment, and commitments eventually translate into work. So let's make a commitment to work.

Audience/Customer Analysis

"Be-a-Spy Theory"

....

Preparation is the key to developing a powerful presentation. It goes without saying you need to know your products cold. We will assume that if you are reading this book, you have reached past that stage. Next you must decide who your customer is and determine why he or she should use your service. Then you must identify your competition. Finally you will need to know if your customer uses your competitor and, if so, why. You can find out this information by asking the right people. In fact, you become a spy. I call it the "Be-a-Spy Theory."

The first target of your intelligence work always is your audience. Who are they, what are their tastes, and how can you communicate with them? Following is a story I tell in my seminars that illustrates how rewarding it can be to know your customer audience.

"Bass Masters" Story

....

I had the opportunity to meet with the vice-president of a company regarding my training and development program. He had agreed to the meeting reluctantly. (Haven't we all met with potential clients who at first didn't much want to meet with us? Of course! Our job is to make them glad they shared their time with us.)

Before I give a presentation such as this, I do my homework. It always helps to preview a client's wants, needs, and expectations.

Not only do I evaluate their professional requirements, but it never hurts to find out about their personal expectations and requirements as well. Frequently, I get this information from someone with whom they work. Other vendors and secretaries usually are very helpful.

I telephoned my client's office assistant on Friday, introduced myself, and said I had an appointment with her employer the following Monday. I told her I always liked to tailor my presentations to meet the specific needs of my client. I asked her if she could tell me a little about him. She said, "Terri, I wish I could help you, but I'm new here, and the only thing I know about him is that he loves bass fishing." Her other telephone started to ring, and she promptly hung up.

I thought—bass fishing? Interesting, but it is not a lot to go on. What do I know about bass fishing? Nothing. So I checked my sourcebook of subject experts and placed a fast call to my father. "Dad, what can you tell me about bass fishing?"

He said, "Absolutely nothing, but I do know there is a TV show on Sundays called 'Bass Masters.' Maybe if you watch that you can get a few tips." Great, I thought sardonically. What a way to spend my Sunday. As the show's scheduled time approached, I sat down in front of the TV prepared to take notes with pencil and pad. My lucky stars—it was a double "Bass Masters" Sunday! I got to watch two episodes with Jimmy Houston. For those of you who don't know, he is the fishing world's equivalent to Donahue. Ol' Jimmy walked me through practically the entire "Bass Masters" lifestyle.

When the program was over, I wondered how I would tie this information into my presentation. My client's greeting gave me the motivation I needed to put my research to work: "Miss Sjodin, I'm very pressed for time, so we're really going to have to hurry this up." (Hasn't this happened to you before? A prospect shortens the originally scheduled appointment time causing you to rush and change your plan of attack?)

I thought, well, fine, there goes my chance to develop rapport. After getting seated, I asked him whether he had an enjoyable weekend. "It was productive," he said, "but not much fun."

I replied, "You know, I spent my weekend the same way. I've been doing so much traveling I haven't had time to do laundry. Sunday I finally got it all out of the dryer. I plopped it on the floor in front of the TV and started folding. The TV already was on, but I had left my remote control on the other side of the room. I was still exhausted so I decided not to bother standing up to get it. Instead, I just sat there watching what was already on; I'm sure you never heard of it—a show called 'Bass Masters'?"

Suddenly, instead of a busy executive, I was talking to a little boy. He became animated, his eyes lit up, and he said, "'Bass Masters?' I watch that show all the time. Yesterday was a double 'Bass Masters' Sunday!"

We sat there for awhile and talked about fishing and eventually got down to business. We had a delightful conversation, and, fortunately, I was able to close a sizable contract.

The irony of the story is, while the client started off by limiting my time, he wound up allowing me more than an hour and a half to give my presentation. He even proffered an invitation to go on a fishing trip with his family. My investment in a telephone call to his secretary and an hour or so watching a fishing program paid off handsomely.

If we do our homework on the personal as well as the professional wants, needs, and expectations of our clients, it makes our presentations much more interesting to our prospects, and we have more fun delivering them. At the same time we create rapport, we establish customer loyalty. People appreciate it when someone spends the time to show a genuine interest in the areas which excite them. Harvey Mackay's book, *Swim with the Sharks Without Being Eaten Alive,* goes so far as to include a questionnaire for developing a personal profile of information on each client.

Eventually, someone is going to catch you making inquiries about matters they may perceive to be outside the course of normal business. Should this happen, simply tell him, "Mr. Jones, you are absolutely right. You caught me! I was doing my homework, but I promise you this: I will put as much energy and effort into maintaining your business as I have put into obtaining your business from the word 'go.' I hope this is the kind of person you want working with you on your transactions." Do you think people are going to be upset when you come back with a response like this? Not at all—they want someone who is willing to hustle in order to get their business. THIS RESPONSE WORKS EVERY TIME.

Ask For Information

Finding out information about a customer or group of clients frequently requires only that you ask. Usually it takes just a couple of minutes. Before an appointment, I will call and say, "Ms. Jones, this is Terri Sjodin. I'm calling to follow up with you and confirm our appointment for 3 P.M. today. I'm trying to do some research so my presentation can meet your specific needs. May I ask you a few quick questions? They will take only about two minutes. If you help me, I can tailor my presentation to meet your specific requirements."

People usually agree and are even more interested in working with me because I am custom-tailoring my sales presentation to their individual circumstances. It often can even be another way to impress them with my service. The converse of this is to spend the first ten minutes talking about something they already know. That is an unforgivable waste of your client's time and very costly for you.

Performing A Competitive Analysis

Not only do you need to know as much as you possibly can about your client, you need to learn about your competition. Once you know who you are up against, you can figure out if your prospect uses their product or service.

The key question here is, why do they use them? The answer will give you information about adapting your presentation to the client's needs. Let's face it: Everyone wants to know what the competition is doing. Football teams even send each other video-tapes so both sides can prepare better for upcoming games.

Identify The Competition

After spending time in any industry, you will begin to know your competition. If you call on someone who has just bought from another salesperson, say, "Oh really? Whom did you purchase it from?" Eventually there will be certain names that you hear repeatedly.

How Do You Measure Up?

▼

List your company's strengths and weaknesses. Develop a strategy to promote the former and minimize the latter.

▲

Having a picture of the competition and a list of the firm's products and services, you begin your competitive analysis. That means you take a hard look at how you measure up in the marketplace. It is your responsibility to find out what makes your competitors unique and why they are getting sales that should be going to you.

Find out how your product is superior to your competition's and where theirs can beat yours. List your company's strengths and weaknesses. Develop a strategy to promote the former and minimize the latter. Figure out how best to offset the advantages held by your competitor. You may want to start doing a few of the things that have created a positive reputation for the other firm. Emulating your competitor's strengths may be necessary to improve your marketplace standing. Why reinvent the wheel?

Service: A Competitive Checklist

Despite the outcome of your competitive analysis, there is one area you can always control: service. Measure how accurate you are, how friendly you are, and whether you do follow-up work. You can completely control these as well as your enthusiasm. They all count heavily (particularly your enthusiasm) in your client's decision whether to work with you or someone else. Always share your personal enthusiasm or passion with the client regarding why you work in your chosen profession. Passion and enthusiasm are contagious and will make people want to work with you long term.

Achieving Credibility

We like to think of ourselves as trustworthy and believable. However, the undeniable profit we receive from convincing someone to buy from us makes us suspect in the eyes of the client. Combine this with a profession whose history is replete with ethical breaches, and you begin to realize why it is terribly important to establish credibility.

Personal And Information Credibility

Your customer will evaluate both you and your information before deciding whether to believe you. Enhancing the credibility of both will help you be more persuasive. I can't overemphasize the importance of sounding believable. If your prospects do not believe in you or what you are saying, they will have to be positively desperate before buying what you are selling.

If you do not positively believe in what you are selling or the service you represent, it will become apparent. Find something else that you can feel personally confident about representing. Your feelings must be aligned with your message.

Major Speech Supports

Credibility is essential to the sales professional, particularly in today's competitive marketplace. Sincerity is the true driver of credibility, yet a sales professional can enhance how convincing his talk sounds by employing what we call "speech supports." Not only will these enhance your credibility, but they will make your presentation sound so interesting you will dazzle your audience. Here is a list of the eight major speech supports.

1. Anecdote (story)
2. Analogy
3. Definition
4. Example
5. Statistics
6. Testimonial
7. Hypothesis
8. Rhetorical Question

Speech supports when documented and used appropriately can give your presentation the credibility achieved otherwise only by personally knowing your client. A speech replete with a variety of supports sounds solid. Documentation gives it credibility. Let's discuss each of the supports briefly so you understand what they are and how they work.

Anecdote

Among the most effective tools in your kit is the anecdote, a short, often humorous story, either real or fictitious. The anecdote allows you to take your message outside the business context with an illustration anyone can understand. It entertains the listener and makes your point memorable. Using an anecdote, such as the "Bass Masters" story, also makes you, the speaker, seem warm-hearted, down-to-earth, and likable.

Analogy

Analogy is the comparison of similar characteristics found in dissimilar circumstances. You might draw an analogy between an artery in a patient who has arteriosclerosis and a mountain stream gradually freezing in winter. Analogies are effective in explaining new material to your listeners because they provide them with reference points they already understand. Salespeople often explain new products and services to prospective customers. Analogies prove useful in bridging the gap between the old and new.

Definition

Most of us already know that a definition is a statement of precise meaning or significance. Using definitions in a presentation can enhance the speaker's credibility. The client perceives the salesperson to be knowledgeable. Using a definition also reduces the chance for miscommunication.

Definitions may be important when you are using technical terms from a given industry. Or other terms you have to use could be colloquial and will need to be defined for your audience. Those who already know the definition will suddenly begin to feel a part of your world, thus enhancing your credibility. Definitions promote the customer's understanding of your meaning. They lead the customer toward seeing things the way you need them to be seen in order for you both to move forward.

Example

An example is one representative from a larger group. We often use examples to clarify general ideas. They may describe benefits or reduced risk. Frequently we use examples to show how something can be used. They might show how to avoid a problem that could take place in the future. You can use examples to describe situations that likely will happen if the client doesn't use your product or service. (Another way to reinforce a harm.) You may want to illustrate the positive feelings or benefits the client will receive from your product. Specifics show how the product can increase pleasure, reduce pain, save money or time.

Statistics

We think of statistics as meaning numbers. More broadly, statistics is the system of mathematics associated with organizing and interpreting numerical data. Using statistics is a highly effective way of ensuring what you say is credible. Yet the impact is dependent upon how dramatic the numbers are. Too many statistics will put your audience to sleep. A good statistic, followed up by a good anecdote or testimonial, will make a strong impression.

Testimonial

When a statement testifying to a particular truth or fact is delivered formally or written down, we call it a testimonial. When we incorporate testimonials within our presentation, we have the weight of another person's reputation reinforcing what we are claiming.

A testimonial says, "Look, these people were nervous, just as you are," or "These people had concerns, just as you do. They went ahead and did it anyway. Now look how happy they are. They even wrote me a letter of reference." The testimonial carries only as much weight with your prospect as the person who signed it. It is important therefore that a testimonial be appropriate.

Hypothesis

The hypothesis is an assumption we postulate to further our argument. We ask, "What if we could prove how this machine will pay for itself in six months? Would you buy it?" We create a hypothetical situation to explain our point.

Rhetorical question

Frequently, a salesperson will want to ask the customer a rhetorical question—a question for which the answer is so obvious it needn't be stated. I might ask, "How many of you have heard your clients say, 'I want to think about it'?"

Such questions help create rapport with the audience. They provide a common bond by showing you both are salt of the earth. Rhetorical questions say, "I'm a good person to listen to because I've been where you have been. I know the things you experience daily. I also can provide you with advice on other things to do in the future." This type of image gives you credibility.

Twelve Emotional Factors That Sell

People are inherently emotional and motivated by positive emotion. Knowing how to uncover the emotional factors that will move your listeners can be your greatest asset in persuasive communication. Following is a list of twelve factors, often employed today in the field of advertising, which are highly effective in all sales presentations.

1. Love of romance
2. Urge of quality
3. Comparison of value
4. Pride of possession
5. Joy of attractiveness
6. Thrill of enthusiasm
7. Pleasure of prestige
8. Security of durability
9. Charm of desirability
10. Elation of suitability

11. Virtue of efficiency
12. Relish of satisfaction

Let me describe a few of these so you will recognize them when you see them and later be able to employ them in your presentations.

The love of romance is commonly the underlying theme for perfume ads and can be found driving certain travel advertisements. Advertisers use people's love of romance to sell just about anything that consumers find appealing.

The urge of quality also is seen in consumer advertising, particularly of automobiles. American automobile manufacturers pride themselves on the luxury interiors they offer and want to make sure consumers believe the cars are as reliable as their overseas counterparts.

Supermarkets are constantly asking shoppers to compare the value they get at one store with that of another. Stretching the housewife's food dollar is a national priority and has great appeal as an advertising theme.

Builders and real estate companies use the pride people feel in home ownership to attract business.

A few others commonly seen include...

1. Health clubs promoting the joy of attractiveness
2. Amusement parks selling the thrill of enthusiasm
3. European luxury automobiles selling the pleasure of prestige
4. Hand-tool manufacturers appealing to the security of durability
5. Travel companies and airlines promoting vacations and ski trips through the charm of desirability
6. A highly advertised men's clothier expressing the elation of efficiency
7. Fax machines, car phones, and microwaves playing to the virtue of efficiency

8. Restaurants often appeal to the relish of satisfaction in promoting specialty menu items...

Developing A Creative Sales Imagination

Among the most frequently overlooked instruments in the sales professional's repertoire is creative imagination. Whoever said sales doesn't demand originality? Conceiving effective, persuasive presentations for different audiences requires tremendous creative energy. While everyone has different levels of talent, people are creative by nature, and creativity can be enhanced like any other skill. It takes initiative and self-discipline.

Two Sources For Ideas

There are only two places from which ideas can come. You either can borrow them from someone else or originate them on your own. Most good ideas are a synthesis drawn from both sources. The renowned jurist, Oliver Wendell Holmes, wrote that an idea often is improved after being transplanted into the mind of another person. Improving upon someone else's idea is a creative and acceptable way to develop your own presentation style.

The important things are to be memorable and to be unique. Using your creative imagination to employ the above speech supports means developing your own anecdotes and corroborating material to support your argument. The source for these often will be everyday life. Using your own personal stories allows your clients to know you better. Such stories are usually very interesting to listeners.

Bag Lady Story

....

One of my favorite stories for seminars is about an adventure in a fast-food restaurant that involves a contest of wills with an old, shabby-looking bag lady. I tell listeners that she sits down and begins eating my food after I get up to get cream for my coffee. After being rebuffed trying to claim ownership of a sandwich that no one in her right mind would want any longer, I return to the counter and charitably order another meal.

Playing on people's occasional, yet secret and socially unacceptable, feelings of stinginess, I confess to taking the old woman's bag when she leaves for the restroom. I describe a second confrontation which ensues when the woman tries to retake her belongings. My belligerent response only mirrors hers. The story paints an absurd picture of humanity: both of us fighting tooth and nail over petty and essentially worthless items.

The effect of the story, however, is such that whenever I tell it, everyone in the room gives me their heart-stopping attention. At the end, they even want to know what was in the woman's bag. "Baloney," I confess—"just like the story."

Everyone laughs and is relieved that I didn't really get into a tug of war with a helpless old lady. But they are entertained and remember the story—and, hopefully, me along with it. I have their attention, and, for a sales professional in a competitive market, that is extremely important. If you are unable to get and maintain someone's attention, you can't sell them your product or service. Conversely, if you make yourself memorable, you have taken the first step toward achieving a customer commitment.

The best anecdotes and stories, part of a sales professional's tool kit, are usually from the common occurrences of everyday life. If you run out of personal tales, try looking in *Chicken Soup for the Soul*, a group of more than one hundred heartwarming stories written and compiled by Jack Canfield and Mark Victor Hansen.

Twelve Keys To Developing Imagination

Here is a list of twelve keys to help develop a creative imagination.

1. Establish a creative environment (where your energy and potential for growth are released)
2. Read books
3. Listen to tapes
4. Read newspapers, journals, and magazines
5. Create a brainstorming group
6. Find a role model
7. Attend courses, workshops, seminars, and conferences
8. Watch TV and movies, and go to comedy shows
9. Evaluate other speakers
10. Conduct customer and competitor interviews
11. Join professional associations or committees
12. Invite a mentor to lunch or dinner

Cellophane Ceiling

Being creative means expanding your horizons. You may find as you begin to do this that some people around you may send signals that they like you just the way you are—even if there is room for improvement. In fact, as you begin to achieve consistent success and profits, hanging on to your old colleagues can be a problem. Just be aware of what I call the cellophane ceiling. That is the invisible roof you bump your head against when you try to set the higher goals necessary to grow and prosper.

This ceiling is created as associates and sometime friends say things like: "Why are you working so much? Are you a workaholic?" Or: "I can't believe you're so motivated by money. I'm not going to slave for the dollar; I want to enjoy life!" Be aware of the cellophane ceiling and try to break through it. Once you do, you will establish a new peer group with new standards, higher goals, and bigger dreams.

Michael Jeffreys, a colleague, trainer, and noted public speaker, describes the phenomenon by telling a story about crabs. He observes that if you put one crab in a pot, it will escape. However, if you put several crabs in a pot, none can climb to freedom. Jeffreys says that as soon as one starts to scale the side of the pot, all the other crabs grab it and drag it down. If you find yourself in an environment that isn't uplifting, ask yourself if you are sitting in a bucket of crabs.

Use The Library

One of the best ways to expand your world is the classic way: read a book. In fact, read lots of books. Read as many books as you can. I know that sounds unrealistic for most people in this fast-paced world of careers, children, and television, but reading will give you an edge. Being more knowledgeable and articulate than your competition will pay off in increased sales. Get a library card if you don't already have one. That alone will put you in the select group of Americans who take advantage of one of today's best education/entertainment values. After all, library books are lent to the public free of charge.

Listen To Audiotapes

There are thousands of books available on audiotape and a few stores that specialize in these terrific motivational tools. Tapes are available at the library also. You can buy tapes often for less than the price of the book, and they are great in the car when you are stuck in traffic. They also are available through mail order.

Subscribe To Periodicals

Subscribe to a newspaper and read it every day. It is important to stay informed so you can discuss with your clients what is happening in the world. Current events are ideal for developing analogies you can use in your presentations. Subscribe to your industry's leading trade magazine. Most executives read these cover to cover and base business decisions on the information they contain. Cut out articles which may be of general interest to your client.

Form A "Think Tank"

Assume a leadership role and create a brainstorming group. Get together with the people in your company or industry and think of as many harms as you can to use in your presentations. Also include prospecting ideas that work and identify those that don't. There are thousands of ideas you can develop through your think tank.

Look For A Role Model

Finding a role model will make it much easier for you to achieve your goals. Such a person already has covered the territory you want to traverse. Having a ready-made map will save you untold time.

Go To Shows

One of the most frequently discussed topics of conversation is the latest hit movie. People talk about what was on television, but you can beat that if you attend a few comedy shows. These provide outstanding material for your presentations. A great way to get people's attention is with a good joke they haven't already heard. Comedians have great one-liners that will add a spark to your presentation and help make it memorable. Just make sure the material is appropriate for your audience.

Hear The Pros
....

Attend speeches and sales presentations delivered by your competition and other industry leaders. If they are good, they probably spent a lot of time and energy developing their skills. You can learn a lot through analyzing how they speak. There is nothing like a live performance to serve as a free training seminar.

Be Blunt: Ask Questions
....

Conducting interviews with customers or competitors means that you go out and actively ask questions about areas of interest with which you should be familiar. It relates to the "Be-a-Spy Theory."

Network Heavily
....

Don't be intimidated by those membership fees that associations charge; join anyway. The dinners and get-togethers are an excellent way to keep up both with the people and the issues relevant to your industry. Networking in these groups is also an excellent way to scout new job opportunities.

Pick Up The Tab
....

Someone you meet through these associations might be interesting enough to invite to lunch or dinner. Such informal meetings can allow you the opportunity to speak in depth with a recognized leader in your field. The information you learn will be well worth the price of a meal. Sharing in the experiences of someone who knows the ropes can save you a great deal of time and money.

In the next chapter, "How to Build a Speech," we will explore the specific techniques you will use to compile all of these tools into an effective, memorable presentation.

Chapter 6

How to Build a Great Presentation

Organizing

With all of the tools at your disposal, you are now ready to begin building your sales presentation. Learning how to organize a talk is easy when you understand the formula. Delivering it with the skill of an eighteenth century orator will take a little more time, but, with practice, you will be able to accomplish that too.

Skilled organization of your argument, deft use of speech supports and transitions, and a clear call to action will make your message irresistible to your audience. You can outline your presentation, write it out word-for-word, or do both. However, you should use a pencil and paper (or word processor) as you develop your ideas. Let's take a look at just how you will build your first truly dazzling presentation.

Signposting

One of the techniques for successful delivery is called "signposting." This means using phrases to let the audience know where you are going with your presentation. It is a way to provide a mental road map to listeners so they can better understand what you say. A signpost gives advance notice of the direction you are taking so that when you get there, your audience will understand you and be ready for the next point.

Writing The Introduction

In grammar school we learned that the introduction to an essay is a single paragraph. That is fine for youngsters, but actually there are four distinct elements within the introduction to a presentation.

First is a bold statement to attract attention. This is a statement that everyone can understand. It should have a universal context. Frequently it is followed by an "anchor," a way to unify the audience and provide a point of common reference. The larger and more diverse the group, the more challenging it becomes to find an effective anchor. Nevertheless, most groups have something in common. When giving a one-on-one presentation, you should be able to determine what you have in common with your client or prospect.

Credibility Enhancer

Next you should include a sentence or two to enhance your credibility. This can be a statistic, a published fact from an authoritative journal, or a quotation by an authority or famous person.

Making It Important

Follow up with a statement to promote the importance of what you are about to say. Why does your client need to react now? What evidence, scientific or otherwise, can you provide that will convince this person that you are about to say something important?

Background Statement

Fourth comes a background statement. This gives your listeners further reason to pay attention to what you have to say. It sets the context for your claims from a historical perspective and helps establish you as an authority.

Transition

These four elements are followed by a smooth transition designed to take the listener into the body, or main part, of the presentation.

Writing The Body

For the sales professional, the body needs to answer three questions:
1. Why should clients work with you?
2. Why should they work with your company?
3. Why should they do it now?

Each of these body points should have five sections:
1. Your argument stating what you want to say or prove
2. Your sources of justification
3. The reasons why your argument will work
4. What risk the prospect will face if he or she doesn't work with you (a harm)
5. The features and benefits of your product or service

The final section is followed by a transition to the next body point—why the prospect should work with your company. A transition separates this segment from the third and last point—why he or she should do it now.

Conclusion

You may have guessed that once you have finished support-ing all three of your body points you would wrap this up with a conclusion. However, the conclusion is not quite as simple as we remember it from school. It has up to five distinct sections:

1. Summary of the information already presented
2. Appeal for your listener to take action
3. Statement of your personal intent (what specific steps you will take to move the transaction forward)
4. Reference back to your introduction (to close with strength)
5. Powerful new story to emphasize your point (optional)

Close

Every presentation must have a close. Your close is the spe-cific call to action—what your client has to do in order to complete the transaction. For example, this could be signing the contract or setting the next appointment time.

Persuasive Presentation Expanded Outline

What follows is a basic outline for persuasive presentations. After reviewing it, develop a talk to deliver during your next sales presentation. Use the blank outline forms printed on subsequent pages to help organize your ideas.

Introduction

Statements to:
1. Grab the audience's attention
2. Focus that attention (short, preferably humorous personal story or quotation)
3. Enhance your credibility of purpose (your goals for the relationship)
4. Make what you say important (why your client should listen to you)
5. Provide background and a...
6. Signpost (to tell them where you are going and what your three points will be)

Transition

Body (typically has three points)

In the body you will build the overall "argument" of why a business transaction needs to be completed. You list separate "points." Each one has its own argument.
1. Why your prospects should work with you
2. Why they should work with your company
3. Why they should act now

Body Point 1

Explain why your prospects should work with you (as an individual); think of the three most important reasons.
1. Your argument (what you want to prove or say)
2. Sources of justification
3. Good reasons why your argument works
4. The harm (what risk they will take if they don't work with you)
5. Your own list of features and benefits

Transition–Body Point 2

Give a rundown of why they should work with your company.
1. Your argument (what you want to prove or say)
2. Sources of justification
3. Good reasons why your argument works
4. The harm (what risk they will take if they don't work with your company)
5. Your company's features and benefits

Transition–Body Point 3

Tell your clients why they should act now.
1. Your argument (what you want to prove or say)
2. Sources of justification
3. Good reasons why your argument works
4. The harm (what risk they will take if they don't do it now)
5. Features and benefits of immediate action

Transition–Conclusion

1. Summary of information
2. Appeal to take action
3. Statement of personal intent (what specific steps you will take to move the transaction forward)
4. Reference back to the introduction (to close with power)
5. New story to emphasize your point (optional)

At this point, you may want to answer questions.

Close

Now comes your specific call to action. What is it you want your audience to do as a result of your presentation?

Typical examples of options you might offer your client at the close of your presentation include:

1. Signing the contract
2. Setting the next appointment time

If the client won't make the commitment right now and sign on the dotted line, it is important to produce your calendar and set a future appointment date. Don't let the client put you off until later if you can possibly avoid it.

Making this type of an outline in advance of your presentation is essential. Benefits are so great that I constantly stress them to clients who go through our training programs. They include:

1. Providing clarity and control of the information
2. Preventing speaker from straying off course
3. Allowing a chance for you to share your knowledge, thus establishing your credibility
4. Promoting audience interaction and encouraging them to think of questions and objections (Also helps audience to formulate positive images and set personal objectives.)
5. Helping the client (or audience) retain more information due to the clear, logical format
6. Helping to build a logical case for why the client should work with you
7. Helping map the course of your presentation so you know where to put stories and illustrations (These contribute to making clear and memorable points resulting in a more persuasive and polished presentation.)
8. Ensuring your overall presentation will be professional

The blank outline form that follows is for planning and practicing your next talk. You may want to make copies of these forms or input them into your computer. That way, it will be easier to develop a new outline to meet the needs of each individual client. The more often you make an outline, the easier it gets.

Persuasive Presentation Practice Outline

Introduction
1. _____
2. _____
3. _____
4. _____
5. _____
6. _____

Transition

_____

Body
1. _____
2. _____
3. _____

Body Point 1
1. _____
2. _____
3. _____
4. _____
5. _____

Transition

_____

Body point 2
1. _____
2. _____
3. _____
4. _____

5. _____

Transition

_____

Body Point 3

1. _____
2. _____
3. _____
4. _____
5. _____

Transition

_____

Conclusion

1. _____
2. _____
3. _____
4. _____
5. _____

Close

1. _____
2. _____

Sample Persuasive Presentation Outline

I. Scenario

Imagine a board of trustees is bringing in three investment management organizations to evaluate and select a new investment advisor. Each management organization will be given thirty minutes to present a general overview of its company. Your company has been selected as one of the five finalists under consideration. Your competitiors are not disclosed. You find out you have been selected to deliver the presentation on behalf of your company twenty-four hours prior to the actual meeting. The outcome of this meeting will determine the two finalists who will be invited back to deliver a second, more specific presentation.

II. Audience Analysis

Audience: the members of the board of trustees, a typically conservative group
Audience size: eight to twelve
Average age range: thirty to sixty-five
Male/Female ratio: 60 percent male and 40 percent female
Attitude of audience: marginally satisfied with current investment advisor
How informed is audience: experts in their vocation but novices in the investment field

III. Logistical information

Facility: meeting room at a college campus
Visual aids: Overhead projector and screen are available. You may also use handouts and flip charts or white board. All

other materials you will need to provide.

Time: thirty minute presentation with an additional fifteen minutes following for Q&A.

Your speaking position: determined at the meeting

Speaker: Ryan Kelly, Spectrum Asset Management Inc., Newport Beach, California

On the following pages, you will find two sample presentation outlines for your review. The first is a Short Presentation Outline which will help you to lay out the basics or core skeleton of a presentation. The second is a Long Presentation Outline, which provides a more detailed look at a comprehensive presentation. Both versions of the outline are effective depending on your comfort level with the material and the amount of practice you commit to the presentation prior to its delivery.

Note: Every argument does not need to have a harm. And every body point does not need to have three subpoints. Use your own judgment and personalization. Try new approaches. Use your creativity.

Short Presentation Outline

I. Introduction

A. Grab attention: tulip analogy
B. Focus attention with short story: captain-eating-the-onion tale
C. Goals for the relationship: to earn their business and to advise clients through knowledge, research, and experience
D. Why should they listen to you?
   1. We truly have a unique advantage to meet your specific needs. There are thousands of investment management

organizations and opportunities. You need to select just one. So why Spectrum Asset Management?

a) We educate you. We help you understand what you don't know.

b) We are a David in a world of Goliaths working for you.

c) Provide background: expand with two illustrations, the issues listed above.

d) Sign post: tell them where you are going and what your three points will be.

    1) Why should they work with Ryan Kelly?

    2) Why should they work with Spectrum Asset Management?

    3) Why should they do it now?

II. Body

A. Point 1: Why Ryan?

  1. As a principal in this firm, I have a vested interest in your success. If you don't do well, I don't do well.

  2. I dump the trade talk: I use simple communication that is clear, concise, direct, and in plain English, so you understand everything that is going on with your portfolio.

  3. When I say we provide more than just our core service, we really do.

B. Point 2: Why Spectrum Asset Management?

  1. Brief company overview: to provide solid foundation and general familiarity with organization

  2. We outperform our competition in terms of:

    a) Customization

    b) Service

    c) Price

    d) Defense strategies

C. Point 3: Why now? Why should you switch to working with Spectrum Asset Management versus your current asset management company–now?
   1. We protect and defend your principal, the second you become a client, through nonemotional exit strategies.
   2. We provide solid growth strategy.
   3. We protect you even in the worst of situations.

III. Conclusion

A. Quickly review the key points of the presentation.
B. Appeal to take action: Ask for the opportunity of a second appointment.
C. Statement of personal intent: The goal of the second meeting would be to roll up your shirt sleeves and create an action plan and implement an investment strategy.

IV. Close

Ask how much money they are willing to commit in an initial advance. Have them sign a contract or set up the next appointment time.

Long Presentation Outline

I. Introduction

A. In Holland in 1636 one rare tulip cost four bushels of wheat, eight pigs, twelve sheep, five kegs of beer, one thousand pounds of cheese, a bed, a fine suit, and a silver cup.
B. Imagine the following story: That same year, the captain of a ship carrying foreign cargo sees an interesting looking onion that he thinks looks out of place among the fine silks they are transporting. The captain eats the onion with his lunch. When the ship arrives on shore, the captain is thrown

in jail for almost a year for eating a tulip that would have fed and paid for the captain's ship and crew for a year. If the captain had known the value of the tulip, he surely would not have eaten it. The following year that same tulip had lost 95 percent of its value and would trade for only the cost of one sheep.

II. Main Point of Presentation

A. To understand your responsibility as a board member is to act as the captain of your ship, and your greatest concern is to protect and increase your investment portfolio. At Spectrum we know which tulips not to eat, how many sheep it should cost to buy a tulip, and when to sell your tulips for the greatest return on your investment. We want to represent you and your financial interests. Our goal is to earn your business and construct a strategy designed for your specific needs based on our research and experience and your comfort level.

III. My Statement Which Makes What I Say Important

A. We truly have a unique advantage to meet your specific needs. Explanation: There are thousands of investment management organizations and opportunities. You need to select just one. So why Spectrum Asset Management?
   1. We educate you. We help you understand what you don't know. (short film, three minutes)
   2. We are a David in a world of Goliaths working for you. How many of you have heard the tale of David vs. Goliath?
      a. Illustration: Two opposing forces were to meet on the field of battle. Good guys were from the west. The bad guys from the east. As was the custom of the day the two opposing forces would often choose a champion to represent them in battle. Goliath from the east was

a giant of tremendous strength and size. He drove
such fear into his opponents from the west that not
one of the west's best warriors came forward because
they were certain to meet death. But after some time a
young sheep herder came forward and said he would
fight the giant named Goliath from the east. As the
two met on the battlefield the giant Goliath laughed at
the young man before him. But, as we all know, David
took out his sling and rock and waved it above his
head and let his rock go, and he slayed Goliath. In the
investment business there are a lot of Goliaths. We are
David working for you in a world of Goliaths.

IV. Signpost

A. My goal is to provide a brief presentation on how our company, Spectrum Asset Management, can meet your investment management organization needs. Initially, I would like
to tell you a little bit about myself. Secondly, I would like to
share with you the unique benefits of working with our company. Finally, I would like to discuss the advantages of working with Spectrum now.

V. Why Ryan?

A. As a principal in this firm, I have a vested interest in your
success. If you don't do well, I don't do well. However, what
does the standard broker get when he/she gives bad advice?
A commission (harm). (Expand.) If you do well, I do well
because I'm an owner. (Explanation and discussion of features and benefits of working with the principal of the firm
versus a standard investment manager.)
B. I dump the trade talk: I use simple communication that is
clear, concise, direct, and in plain English, so you understand

everything that is going on with your portfolio. (No industry jargon.) In addition, in our business there are two types of people: those who tell you what you want to hear and those who tell you wht you should hear (harm). (Explanation of why when you work with Ryan you get the straight talk you need to make effective decisions.)

C. When I say I provide more than just our core service, I really do, at no extra charge. I am a resource to you. (Argument/Point) I can provide advice on the quality of a portfolio, transferring stock certificates, determining the value on an arcane stock, estate planning, help in Leverage Buy-Out, and setting up a Charitable Remainder Trust. (Explain with features and benefits.)

VI. Why Spectrum?

A. We're unique because we specialize in individual portfolio management accounts, in the half-million to twenty million dollar range. (Argument/Point)

B. What does that mean to you? Because of our specialization, we can outperform our competitors in customization, service, and price as well as defensive strategies. For example, imagine that the goal of your investment advisor is to bake you a cookie. The Goliaths of this business roll out the dough and then take out a cookie cutter and make the same shaped cookie for every one. What the Davids do is make custom cookies. You need a gingerbread man, that's what we cut. You need a cake that's what we bake. You need something that says "Happy Birthday son," that's what you get. They are serving you plain vanilla wafers when you need a gingerbread man (harm). At Spectrum, we provide our clients custom baked cookies at a better price than our competitor's mass produced Oreos. Evidence: We currently provide this customized service for a number of clients. If you would like to speak to them, we would be happy to arrange for it.

C. We are strong defensive players. (Argument/Point) If you have a million dollars and it's worth $700,000 the next week you don't care what your relative performance is. You care that your money is gone. Our goal is to avoid risk. (Additional Point) So we hit base hits not home runs. Babe Ruth in his day had the most home runs but also had the most strikeouts. In baseball that's fine, but in investments it takes too long to make up lost capital (harm). Hypothetically if you lose 50 percent of your assets you have to make 100 percent to get to even, whereas if you lose 20 percent of your assets you have to make 25 percent which is much more doable. Naturally our focus is on a *zero* capital loss.

VII. Why Now?

A. Why should you switch to working with Spectrum versus your current asset management company–NOW? Everyone gets religion after the devil shows up, why not get it before-hand? Let's say you have a million dollars and six months from now it's worth $700,000. How would that make you feel? Would have, could have, should have are the three richest men in the world. Sometimes doing nothing can cost you a lot more than taking action (harm), because the time to take action is before things hit the fan. Afterward it's too late.

B. We protect and defend your principal the second you become a client, through nonemotional exit strategies. In our industry, the biggest weakness that individuals and professional investors have is that they are bad sellers. They don't sell when they should. On all of our positions, we have a *sell alert and a sell stop* which ensures that we avoid significant loss, and we take the emotion out of the selling decision. You get the security of protecting your principal with all the advantages of growth potential, which means less risk to you the client.

C. We provide solid, conservative growth strategy. Unfortunately, the majority of our clients come to us after they have already suffered a great deal of pain and loss. The reason is because most investment decisions are made reactively versus proactively.

D. Illustration: In 1994, all of Spectrum Asset Management's institutional accounts made money. In contrast, if the County of Orange had been a client under the same management strategy we calculated, it would have made money instead of losing 12.7 billion dollars, which caused its bankruptcy. We protect you even in the worst of situations. The year 1994 was the worst in the government bond market since 1927. However, the government bond mutual fund managed by Spectrum finished number three in the country, which means that even in the worst of situations, our clients maintained their principal. We protect our client's hard- earned dollars. We'd like to do the same for you.

VIII. Conclusion

A. Summary of Information Given (Quickly review key points of presentation.)
B. Appeal to take action
   1. (Ask for their business.) Ask for the next appointment time to present a more in-depth case.
C. Statement of Personal Intent
   1. (What you will do to carry forth the business relationship?) Share how you will personally roll up your shirt sleeves to create a customized action plan to meet their specific needs and provide a detailed explanation of how to implement their investment strategy.
D. Reference to Introduction

At Spectrum we are willing to do what it takes to earn your business. We would be honored to represent your account.

IX. Close

A. *What do you want them to do as a result of your presentation? How much money are they willing to commit in an initial advance? Will they sign a contract or set up the next appointment time?*

The Overnight Presentation

A Golden Opportunity

You are at your desk, it is 3:30 P.M., and you have at least a half day's worth of work to do before you go home. Your regional manager walks in.

"Joan, I know this is rather short notice, but I need someone to fill in for me tomorrow morning at the vice-president's staff meeting. I just got called back to headquarters, and my flight leaves tomorrow at 8:30 A.M. Can you help me out?"

"Sure," you reply, eager to please your manager but with little idea of what is involved.

"Okay," she says. "Here's the deal. We have to sell the finance committee on the importance of funding the Bellwether Project. All budget requests must be in by tomorrow. Anything not submitted won't be considered for funding next year. If that happens, the project won't get started for three-and-a-half years. As it is now, it will be more than eighteen months before we can get underway. We couldn't compile the material earlier because the contractor estimates weren't in yet."

"Well, what do I have to do?" you ask, slightly bewildered and a little alarmed that this is a critical presentation for which there is insufficient time to prepare. "Just make sure the committee members understand the project, that they are convinced of its importance, and that all of them believe it will pay for itself over the next five years. It is absolutely vital, as you know. Here are all the materials." She drops eight huge file folders onto your desk. "Thanks, Joan. I won't forget this at your review."

As you watch her disappear around the corner, you think to yourself, "Probably the same 4 percent as last year—I shouldn't get a raise; what I deserve is a promotion!"

Career Boost

Well, this could be your ticket to greener pastures. While it is not a typical sales scenario, we have included a section on the overnight presentation because it occurs frequently in business and may involve a sales presentation. Though you don't have time to produce a colorful videotape, and may not even have time to make view-graphs, you still can put together a convincing oral presentation that will knock the socks off the finance committee and achieve the objectives established by your manager. Considering the authority level of your audience, to say that a good performance before this committee might give your career a boost would be to state the obvious. Before that can happen, however, you will have to impress them.

Getting The Job Done

The secret to a successful overnight presentation lies in carefully planning what to say. Use the outline on the preceding pages, review your facts and source materials, and you may find you can simply fill in the blanks. If you follow the outline, it will see you through to a successful conclusion. The result will be a logical, formulated, and convincing presentation.

I list a series of pointers here so you can get a sense of how to deliver your talk once you get the words written. Keep these guidelines fresh in your mind if you are asked to give an overnight presentation; study them too for general principles that work in everyday selling situations.

Twenty-one Keys To A Powerful Presentation Style

1. Believe in everything you say and represent
2. Set objectives
3. Plan the best approach
4. Establish time limits
5. Craft the introduction carefully
6. Organize your presentation into a logical outline
7. Use humor, anecdotes, stories
8. Select speech supports appropriate to the audience
9. Clearly summarize information
10. Encourage listener participation
11. Ensure all facts and statistics are scrupulously accurate
12. Express vitality with your voice
13. Evaluate the attitudes and needs of your audience
14. Provide enduring conclusions
15. Vary your pace
16. Speak clearly and distinctly
17 Be lively and enthusiastic
18 Be clear when moving from point to point
19. Don't oversell; use a conversational approach
20 Use variation in your vocabulary
21. Find a public speaking role model

(The last key obviously isn't going to help you with an overnight presentation, but it may motivate you to perform better when called upon to deliver the next one.)

Use your creativity and you will be able to deliver an effective extemporaneous presentation with less than a day's notice. With imagination and enthusiasm your delivery may just earn you that promotion you deserve.

Chapter 7

Becoming a Power Speaker

Learning To Soar

Testing Our Theories

We spent the last chapter analyzing how to put together the parts of a powerful presentation. It is a technical job, much like assembling the sections of an airplane. Now in the cockpit, you may suddenly begin to get a little nervous as you start rolling down the runway. Leave the ground? Fly? Are you nuts?

Yes, that is what it is all about. We have just constructed a great flying machine—now it is time to see how it takes to the air.

People get a great sense of exhilaration from giving a talk. They get a great sense of exhilaration from making a sale. Both are competitive activities, and all the rules that apply to competitive sports apply to giving a powerful sales presentation. You can drag along making a sale once every eight or ten presentations, but, even if you can pay your bills that way (which is doubtful), can you handle

> ▼
> You can drag along making a sale once every eight or ten presentations, but, even if you can pay your bills that way (which is doubtful), can you handle that much rejection?
> ▲

that much rejection? You need to get off the ground. You need to be airborne. Your speeches need to be consistent and profitable.

Taking Risks

Everything Has A Price

If there is one thing in life that proves itself repeatedly, it is the old saying, "You don't get something for nothing." You want to be a success? Fine. You are going to have to take risks. Getting up in front of people and putting your heart and soul into your presentation is one of those risks. Earlier we discussed how some people rarely exert themselves. When they fail, they say it doesn't count because they weren't really trying. Thus, they have a reason for failure. Never mind that they are virtually ensuring failure by their lack of commitment.

Managing Anxiety

To give a successful sales presentation you have to invest a great deal of time and energy. You have to be committed to it. Then you have to be willing to take the risk that it might be a success. You would be surprised at how many people are afraid of success. To be a power speaker, you have to have power. To have power, you have to have energy. Where do you get it? You channel your anxiety. Call it fear, call it excitement, call it nervousness—it is the energy you have available before you give a presentation. All you have to do is learn how to manage it.

Everyone Gets Nervous

Among common fears, most people rank public speaking up there with falling out of an airplane. I have seen people become panicky to the point of paralysis during video training sessions. In one session, a woman started crying, and, in another, I thought the man was going to have a heart attack. Certain people are more anxious about giving talks than others. Those who are more prone to being nervous have "high communication-apprehension" personalities. Others have a "low communication-apprehension" makeup. However, even the most callous politician gets a little nervous before making a presentation.

Success Is What Counts

The main thing to remember is that it is perfectly normal to feel nervous before a presentation, particularly if you are putting a lot of yourself into it. And to put on a good show, you have to give of yourself. It doesn't matter how nervous you are. What counts is how successful you are. Did your prospect buy your product? Did you convince your listener of the legitimacy of your point of view?

Your audience determines whether you are successful, and to win their applause you will have to appear polished. When I say someone is polished, I mean he or she has a smooth flow, a strong command of the material, the audience, the environment, the time—they have a presence that is commanding.

On Becoming Polished

First, You Have To Care

You ask, "Terri, this is what we have been leading up to. How do I learn to be polished?"

I see people during training who give presentations that are incredibly sloppy. There are several reasons, and the first one is they simply don't care. They are going to coast, not really trying to look good or sound good. Unfortunately, it's obvious to the audience. In so many words, they are saying to their listeners, "I don't care if I waste your time."

In order to become a polished speaker you must desire to be one—you have to care about how you are perceived. You have to care about your audience, whether it is made up of one or one hundred people.

A Little Knowledge Helps

The second reason people don't give strong presentations is they don't have a clear idea what they should be doing. Nor are they able to see what they actually are doing. They aren't aware of how bad they look or sound. They don't have a vision of how good they could be.

Practice Makes Perfect

The third reason people give poor presentations is that they just haven't committed to enough practice to be able to do it right.

Ingredients Of Achievement

Knowledge, practice, and the will to improve—does that sound familiar? Of course it does. These are the same three qualities necessary to achieve anything worthwhile.

Let's face it. Giving a good presentation is challenging. If it were easy, everyone would be doing it. The opportunity for you as a sales professional, however, is to use this skill to increase your closing ratio—and your income—and to motivate others to act on your ideas. Those are powerful incentives for someone to accept such a challenge. And you will improve significantly if you implement the techniques in this book.

Polish

The subtle quality of a true power speaker is charisma—the mesmerizing charm a person expresses in the presence of another. Charisma comes from self-confidence—the certainty of knowing what is happening and what is about to happen. Self-confidence emerges with polish—control over thought, voice, and appearance. All these characteristics find their common root in individual practice.

Polish is also achieved through your professional/personal etiquette before, during, and after your presentations. For a good reference guide on the subject, read *Corporate Protocol, A Brief Case for Business Etiquette* by Valerie Grant-Sokolosky.

Exercising Control

Despite some commonly held reservations about so-called controlling relationships, you will need to exercise control over your listeners and the immediate situation if you want to be a power speaker. No control, no power. No power, no sale. However, the type of control you are exercising is common to all forms of leadership. The secret to being successful is your credibility. There are five elements you will need to control in order to create the right impression. They are:

1. Dress
2. Body language
3. Facial expressions
4. Eye contact
5. Information

The Importance Of Dress

To be in control, you must be aware of the importance of your dress. When your clients question themselves about how credible you are, the first thing they look at is how you are dressed. A mentor once told me, "Terri, when it comes to business presentations—dress for what you aspire to, not for the position you currently hold."

People often draw conclusions long before we ever have a chance to prove ourselves professionally. In unscientific polling of cold calls, we have found that prospective clients give salespeople only about thirty-seven seconds to create a positive impression. That isn't much time. During role play drills in my workshops, we found if you are giving a one-on-one presentation to a husband and wife you have just over five minutes. A woman typically will determine whether or not she likes you in about seventeen seconds. (Does this explain some of today's dating problems?) Men are a little more generous. They will give a person approximately forty-five seconds.

A woman typically will determine whether or not she likes you in about seventeen seconds.

People frequently judge us upon things that have absolutely nothing to do with our professional ability. The very first characteristic they evaluate is dress. Expensive clothes aren't essential. More important is that our clothes look clean, pressed, and coordinated in color and style. Our image should be appropriate to our message. In corporate America, that frequently means conservative.

Michael E. Gerber, author of *The E Myth*, suggests that the color of your outfit can have a tremendous impact on the success of your sales presentations. He suggests salespeople try the following test for six weeks:

"For the first three weeks wear a brown suit to work, a starched tan shirt, a brown tie (for men), and well-polished brown shoes. Make certain that all the elements of your suit are clean and well pressed. For the following three weeks wear a navy blue suit (three-piece for men, two-piece for women), a good, starched white shirt, a tie with red in it (a pin, a scarf, or a necklace with red in it for women), and highly polished black shoes.

"The result will be dramatic: Sales will go up during the second three-week period! Why? Because, as our clients have consistently discovered, blue suits outsell brown suits! *And it doesn't matter who's in them!*"

The Bachelorette Party

Some business people believe it is important to maintain a consistent and conservative image, even at play. In *Trump: The Art of the Deal,* Donald Trump says he is always dressed for business when he goes out because he never knows whom he might meet. It is something to think about.

Once I shocked a small but important group of clients by appearing in a too-hip outfit at a local nightclub. It was a girlfriend's bachelorette party, and several of us decided we were going to paint the town. We all put on miniskirts and spiked our hair so it stood up high. I wore black stockings, black pump shoes, and a black leather jacket.

We rented a limousine, and the five of us whisked off to the first of a series of night spots. I was just getting into the mood of the place—which means I was mentally in "fun mode" on top of a dance platform—when I looked down and saw a table full of business clients. They had been in a training seminar the previous week. Their jaws all were at the same attitude—wide open. They looked shocked. Needless to say, they could hardly wait until Monday morning to report the incident to their manager. By the time I arrived at my office, I had a half-dozen messages on the answering machine from male clients either chiding or teasing me.

While I was on my own time that evening and just having fun, the incident made me acutely aware of how important dress can be to your business associates—and your career. You never know whom you might run into! If you need help with how to dress, consult the industry bible, *Dress for Success,* by John T. Molloy. While slightly outdated, it can provide a basic guideline for you. My best suggestion, however, is to hire a professional clothing consultant.

First And Last Impressions

For the same reason that it is important to dress appropriately, it is also critical that you create positive first and last impressions. Besides your appearance, your opening remarks will be what people use to form their initial, and often lasting, impressions. Roger Ailes, in his book, *You Are the Message,* notes that research indicates we begin to make up our minds about other people within seven seconds of first meeting them. It is a good idea always to acknowledge your audience and establish your position in relation to them beyond the fact you are about to give a speech. Remember the principle of providing an anchor. As you establish your position, try to create a common link.

Next, capture their attention by saying something that is important to them. Try thinking of something that differentiates you from the thousands of other people who are trying to do the same thing you are.

Nonverbal Communication

In order to create a strong presence you will need to communicate on both a nonverbal and a verbal level. We already have discussed how you will put together the words. Let's take a look at the other messages the audience will receive.

Body Language

Body language is very important to the sales professional and to anyone who is giving a speech. The way you move does three things: it conveys meaning, it influences the audience's attention, and it establishes spatial relationships. Your body naturally wants to gesture. For example, many people gesture with their hands while talking on the telephone even though the person to whom they are talking can't see them. Be certain the movements you use while giving a presentation complement your message, and do not distract from it.

Hands In Your Pockets

During our training sessions we videotape nearly every mistake anyone possibly could make while giving a talk. Each gender has its own peculiar habits. Men have a tendency to keep their hands in their pockets when they speak. It is very common to see them play with their change, play with their keys... What the heck are they doing down there anyway? With hands in pockets and elbows flapping back and forth, some resemble chickens.

Hands Near Your Face

Women often play with their hair or touch their faces. Do you ever cross your arms? That is supposed to mean that you are closed off and not receptive. It isn't always true, but what if your client has heard that myth and then sees you crossing your arms?

One of our students told a story to the class about having a bee fly into his ear. He illustrated the point by sticking his finger right where the bee flew in. This could have been effective if done once. But throughout his talk he kept repeating the demonstration until it appeared compulsive. No matter how many times I interrupted and told him to stop doing it, that little finger would arch back up into his ear. Apparently he felt more comfortable with his finger sticking into the side of his head than he did with it resting at his side—at least when recounting his "bee story."

One, Two, Three—Kick!

Another student must have been a cheerleader in high school because every time she made a point she kicked out her leg. I kept saying, "Betty, stand still." She would say, "I am!" Only after we played back the video and proved to her what she was doing did it register. For laughs we put the VCR on fast-forward, and it looked like a lesson in how to do the cancan.

Are You A Penguin?

Another favorite mannerism is doing what I call the "penguin." That is when a person keeps his arms straight down at his sides but flips his fingers up in unison. Presumably he is trying to keep himself from moving, but the urge isn't completely suppressed. Others do what I call the "spider." That is when the fingers curl into a ball, then slowly fan out in an expression of extreme tension. Both gestures are terribly distracting.

The Robot

The robot often shows up on video. This is the person who moves around in a very stiff way as though all his joints need lubricating—sort of like the Tin Man after the rainstorm in *The Wizard of Oz.*

Pens In Pocket

We often see gestures with a pen. Whether it is a diamond-studded presentation model or a cheap plastic throwaway, a pen is very distracting. One student kept rolling the tip of his tie around his pen as though he were making a crêpe suzette.

Oops! Too Close

Spatial relationships are important to people. It is up to the sales professional to allow the client to set the speaking distance. This guideline applies most definitely in one-on-one situations. If the client invites you closer, then move forward. Make sure you test your spatial parameters with your client, however. Have you ever had a salesperson act too friendly from the start? That can be more offensive than someone who is too standoffish.

Angry? Me?

Sometimes a person's facial expressions become contorted when they are giving a presentation. A man's eyebrows may come together making him look very stern. While some people may interpret this expression as authoritative, others will see it as intimidating.

Try practicing smiling at the beginning and end of your presentation. It doesn't have to be a cheesy, fake smile, just that little human element. Your smile is a great asset. When you begin adding those personal stories and your particular brand of passion to your presentation, a smile will come naturally.

Look Deep Into My Eyes

Eye contact is very important to your listeners. Look directly into the eyes of your client frequently before looking away. If you are addressing a group, look into the eyes of individual members of the audience. It gives the others the feeling you are connecting with everyone in the room. If you are looking over the heads of people in the audience, you won't have eye contact.

Move With Meaning

Remember that your movements convey meaning. There is a big difference between moving with intent and pacing back and forth. Don't be a "dancing Dan," jumping all over the stage. Try shifting your weight at the precise moment you make the change to the next major point in your presentation. Try taking a few steps to the side as you approach a transition or new topic. The audience automatically will refocus its attention and understand, through your movements, you are moving to a new idea.

Nervousness

You Are Perfectly Normal

One of the major inhibitors to improvement is nervousness. A presenter may be so relieved at having completed his or her talk that he or she could not care less whether it was any good. At that moment, it doesn't matter if there is a next time, much less whether it will be better than the last. Two things to remember about nervousness are, first, it is completely normal, and, second, a variation of it likely will stay with you forever.

Preparation Can Relieve Anxiety

If you have ever competed in sports, you know that you always are going to be a little nervous before a game or a race no matter how good you become. The best people in any competitive activity are nervous before an event. Giving a good sales presentation is competitive. The better prepared you are, however, the less nervous you will be.

Symptoms Of Nerves

Let's take a closer look at the symptoms of nervousness and their apparent causes. A dry throat is a sign, as are moist palms, fluttery stomach (even nausea), shortness of breath, and feet that feel like lead. Look in the mirror and see if your face is red. It is probably nerves.

Some Get More Nervous Than Others

Some people get more nervous in front of a group than others. We call these individuals high communication apprehension people. Others are more laid back. These are low communication apprehension people. Each of us has a different personality and will react differently to the same situation. In extreme cases of high communication apprehension, one has to ask oneself if sales is the right business to be in. Not everyone will get used to speaking in public, even one-on-one. That is why some people choose to become librarians.

The main thing is to try public speaking, implement the techniques in this book, and evaluate whether your anxiety starts going down. Most people will adjust to the stress, but not all. The woman who broke down in tears during our training session probably will get over that, but she has a longer road ahead than someone for whom public speaking is effortless.

Causes Of Nervousness

There are different reasons why people feel nervous during a talk. We can point to a few obvious ones:
1. Lack of preparation
2. A general lack of self-confidence
3. Lack of self-confidence about a specific ability

4. Fear of failing
5. Fear of inadequacy
6. Fear of embarrassment
7. Fear of being evaluated poorly

Yet even when all of these issues are put to rest as well as humanly possible, we still find that we are nervous. As we scratch a little deeper for a reason beneath the surface, we realize how terribly exposed and vulnerable we feel in front of a major client or group. We know it is up to us to carry the weight of the entire dialogue.

It is common knowledge that before competition we are filled with contradictory emotions: the fear of failure and the desire for success. There is little question that giving a presentation is exciting. Some have equated it to the adrenaline rush we feel during a romantic arousal. The difference between the nervousness we feel before romance and that which precedes a speech is only that we know how to channel the energy that develops before lovemaking. We can also learn how to channel the energy that develops before giving a presentation.

Success Is What Matters

One important thing to reiterate is that it is not how nervous you are that counts, it is how successfully you deliver your presentation. Being open with the audience about your nervous feelings likely will not further your success. The idea is to make a sale, whether it be a signed contract, a follow-up appointment, or an audience prepared to go out and vote for your candidate. Telling listeners that you are nervous is not going to convince them. It may lead them to believe you are nervous because you are not competent. People believe the opposite of being nervous is feeling confident and, therefore, capable.

Keep It To Yourself

Listeners don't know you are nervous if you don't let them in on the secret. You don't look nervous to them, and they won't know what you don't tell them. Divulging your apprehension before your presentation is not going to help either one of you. If you have to be open about it, tell them afterward. Here are a few do's and don'ts to help you control your anxiety.

Do...

1. Take your time
2. Move to refocus your concentration
3. Aim for variety in gesturing
4. Modulate your voice
5. Allow your body to talk
6. Have a sense of humor about yourself
7. Speak clearly; enunciate each word

Don't...

1. Confess you are nervous
2. Apologize
3. Panic
4. Pace back and forth
5. Cross your arms
6. Fiddle with pens, pencils, papers
7. Rush

And above all else, never...

Be boring!

Remember that when you are nervous, you are under stress. When you are under stress, you are learning new things. As the saying goes, "No pain, no gain." If you aren't nervous and don't feel uncomfortable, you aren't pushing your limits, and you aren't growing.

It's All In Your Delivery

Be Interesting And Entertaining

Control of the way that you say the words in your talk is important. One of the exercises we routinely do during training is to videotape students telling a personal story and then making a business-related presentation. The personal stories always are much more interesting, and it is not because of the subject matter. The difference is that people tell the personal stories with passion. Students change their voice inflection, manipulate their facial expressions, contort their bodies for demonstration purposes, and are interesting and entertaining.

After they see a video of their business talks they often apologize for being boring. It almost goes without saying that if you think you are boring, there is a high probability your audience thinks so too. However, people generally don't like to be corrected for something like talking, which they have been doing all their lives. It is difficult for us to accept the idea that we may need improvement in this very personal area.

We have already talked about bringing in personal stories, anecdotes, and other speech supports, which, in addition to helping your credibility, will make your talk more interesting.

Modulate Your Voice

One of the things that you can do to keep your presentations exciting is to maintain control over the sound of your voice. This is particularly relevant in selling because you should be in tune with your listener anyway. If someone is speaking softly to you, you don't shout at them, you match their tone and volume. Have you ever had the disconcerting experience of having a salesperson yell at you repeatedly after your series of soft-spoken questions? Conversely, if your prospect is loud and aggressive, you need to be more hard-hitting.

Controlling the tone and volume of your voice allows you to make your talk sound more interesting while you stay in touch with your client. Being able to project your voice so that you can be heard is half the battle. Inexperienced speakers frequently don't talk loud enough for everyone in the room to understand them. The tone you use and your vocal variation allow you to project your own personality and to create a positive response whether you are speaking to one or one hundred people.

Here are several exercises that will help your tone and your ability to articulate.

1. Sing in the car and shower (with or without radio)
2. Pretend to speak with an accent (parlez-vous francais?)
3. Practice your talk using different emotional tones, such as love or anger

Above all, be aware of how you sound, and don't hesitate to use a standard tape recorder to practice your talk. Take your tape recorder along on your next one-on-one sales call. None of us sound the same to ourselves as we do to others. If your presentation is boring on the tape, you need to spice it up. I assure you that you will catch deficiencies in your talk that you will want to fix. (Those missteps undoubtedly will act as incentives for you to put your standard objections into manuscript format.) A good book that goes into more detail on this subject is *Power Speak* by Dorothy Leeds.

The Importance Of Good Diction

Another helpful skill in keeping your audience's attention is the use of good diction. Diction relates to both your choice and use of words as well as to how clearly you pronounce them. Good diction is the mark of a well-educated person.

One way to improve your enunciation is to speak more slowly. Most people speak too quickly. One way to slow down is to practice reciting tongue twisters. They remind us of the need to enunciate and force us to slow to a crawl. Here are a few good ones:

> *Theophilus the thistle sifter*
> *While sifting a sifter full of thistles*
> *Thrust three thousand thistles*
> *Through the thick of his thumb.*

> *I stood on the steps of Burgesse's Fish Shop*
> *Mimicking him hiccuping*
> *And welcoming him in.*

> *Silly Sally sits and shells her peas*
> *All day long she sits and shells*
> *And shells and sits*
> *And sits and shells*
> *And shells and sits.*

Remember in giving a talk, even if it is one-on-one, you are assuming the role of an authority. If you mispronounce words, use the wrong word for the intended meaning, and generally display a lack of knowledge, it is going to be difficult to maintain respect. However, everything is relative. The bumbling presentation before one group might sound like the message of a prophet to another. So don't withdraw just because you lack a formal education. Find an audience who appreciates what you have to say.

As you mature and become more knowledgeable, you will be able to impress increasingly sophisticated circles.

Buy And Use A Dictionary

Your best friend in developing good diction is a dictionary. Buy two so you can keep one at the office. Better yet, get three—one for the car. Don't buy the cheap pocket type. They are good only for spelling. Invest in a hard-bound collegiate dictionary that has multiple meanings. Whenever you hear a little voice in the back of your mind that questions whether you are using a word properly, spend the sixty seconds it takes to look it up. (If you can't even find the word, you are misspelling it and probably butchering its pronunciation.) A best-selling book that has helped many people improve their diction and overall fluency with the language is *Thirty Days to a More Powerful Vocabulary* by Wilfred Funk.

Keep 'em Laughing

Note your listeners' reactions as you proceed with your presentation. Try to keep them interested and enthusiastic. You want them happy that they spent their time with you. Have you ever been talking to a group when someone starts to fall asleep? It may not be because you are boring them, it may be because they were up all night for business or personal reasons. However, it is important that you try to rouse them. It is very impressive to clients if you can recapture their attention once they start to slip into oblivion.

Emotional Conclusion

Conclude your presentation with an ending that emotionally drives home your point. Think of your speech supports—stories, anecdotes, humor—think of how you can tie everything you have been talking about together, and think about your call to action.

Preparing for a presentation is similar to getting set for a ski race. Once you are out of the gate, there is no turning back. The pace is quick, the course is slippery, and all eyes are on you—the lone competitor barreling down the slope.

The Warm-up

Before engaging in this type of competitive activity, you will need to do what all athletes do—a warm-up. It is important that you begin your presentation in a relaxed state. I always breathe deeply, close my eyes, and imagine how great my talk will be. I stretch and extend my arms and make circles with my out-stretched hands. I imagine applause at the conclusion of my speech or a smile on my clients' faces when they have signed the contract and made a commitment to the project.

I always eat a light, nourishing breakfast the day of a big presentation. Frequently I practice with tongue twisters. Remember to relax and warm up ahead of your talk, and things will go a lot smoother.

Full Dress Rehearsal

Rehearsals are essential preparation for a good talk. Failure to rehearse says to the client, "I don't care if I waste your time." To prepare properly you have to run through a dress rehearsal at home. That means dressing up in the suit you plan to wear during your presentation and practicing every word.

Turn on your tape recorder and practice your talk until it sounds smooth and convincing. Ask the people in your office to listen to your talk and critique it. Close your eyes and visualize delivering your speech. Imagine the positive response from the listeners. Practice all the words you plan to use so that you are familiar with each one and can say it without stumbling.

Critique Every Presentation

In order to improve, you will have to evaluate every presentation you deliver and identify its strengths and weaknesses. Be your own best critic and evaluate everything you do. Invite comments from others, and let them know that you are looking for criticism as well as the usual pats on the back. Sift through their comments to identify areas where you can improve.

Handling Criticism

When you are criticized more than you care to be, try to let some of it roll off your back. Don't let someone else's knocks break you. Gracefully accept compliments from others. And remember to find a role model, someone who does what you would like to do. The person should be very good at giving presentations and willing to spend a little time helping you. Perhaps you can return the favor by performing some helpful work for him or her.

Visual Aids

We can't leave this section without touching on the role visual aids play in emphasizing your message. They do help the audience to understand the points that you are making. They provide support to the body of your speech. The biggest problem, particularly for sales professionals, is that they tend to make the visual aids the focus of their presentations. As a presenter, you need to remember that you are the star. The visual aids are the bit players. They are there only to enhance your presentation, not to take it over.

To learn techniques for using view-graphs, slides, and charts, consult the book, *How to Prepare, Stage and Deliver Winning Presentations*, by Thomas Leech.

Using An Evaluation Chart

Following is an evaluation chart that you can use or ask a friend to fill in for you to keep track of how successful each of your talks is. Try using it to evaluate the presentations of others. This practice will help you become increasingly sensitive to the various elements of a good sales presentation.

Speaker _____

Topic _____

Content	Excellent	Above Avg.	Average	Poor
Choice of material	❏	❏	❏	❏
Organization	❏	❏	❏	❏
Signposting	❏	❏	❏	❏
Analysis	❏	❏	❏	❏
Relevance to audience	❏	❏	❏	❏
Creation of needs	❏	❏	❏	❏

Performance				
Emotional involvement	❏	❏	❏	❏
Verbal projection	❏	❏	❏	❏
Tone variation	❏	❏	❏	❏
Volume control	❏	❏	❏	❏
Speed control	❏	❏	❏	❏
Clarity	❏	❏	❏	❏

Conviction	❑	❑	❑	❑
Clear call to action	❑	❑	❑	❑
Overall performance	❑	❑	❑	❑

Body Expression

Poise	❑	❑	❑	❑
Audience contact	❑	❑	❑	❑
Gesture/movement	❑	❑	❑	❑
Facial expressions	❑	❑	❑	❑

Comments:

_____

_____

The Nine Biggest Sales Presentation Mistakes And How To Avoid Them

Remember, in today's competitive marketplace, whether selling a product, a service, a philosophy, an idea, or, most importantly, yourself—everybody sells something. An individual's success often depends upon his/her ability to deliver a polished and persuasive presentation. Salespeople spend 80 percent of their time verbally communicating, and many suffer from common shortcomings in their sales presentations that adversely affect their results.

After reviewing the following list of the nine most common sales presentation mistakes, you will be able to evaluate your own performance, then make changes where necessary. Learning to build and deliver more professional presentations can directly impact your bottom-line results. The first four items address content and the last five focus on delivery.

Mistake One–"Winging" It

When you "wing it," it's very common for your presentation to "hop and pop" around all over the place, lacking logical, progressive flow. It takes too long to deliver, and prospects may find it hard to follow. Frequently, you may leave out half the points you want to make, including effective illustrations which bring the presentation to life.

Take time to prepare and practice using a logical outline. Be sure your presentation covers all the points you want to make, clearly and concisely. Don't be afraid to give a copy of the outline to your listener.

Mistake Two–Being Informative Versus Persuasive

It's very easy to deliver an informative rather than persuasive presentation. The reason? A prospect can't say "no" when you're only disseminating information. Remember, it's a teacher's job to be informative, but a salesperson must be persuasive.

Learn how to build a presentation that creates needs rather than just covers the standard needs analysis. Think "proactive" versus "reactive." Design a presentation that anticipates and overcomes objections before they become reasons not to buy. Think like an attorney and build arguments for why a client should work with you and your company and why they should do it now.

Mistake Three–Providing Inadequate Support

Your prospect won't buy into your proposal if you are unable to support your claims. Many people deliver presentations based on opinion rather than logical argument for why a client or prospect should take action. You must be able to prove your case when confronted by the prospect, or you will lose credibility.

Remember to use current examples, statistics, stories, and anecdotes to support your points. Magazines, books, interviews, and other studies can provide you with factual support that can build your case and enhance your credibility, thereby, making it more interesting for your audience to listen.

Mistake Four–Failing To Close The Sale

It's hard to believe, isn't it, but often salespeople still don't close at the end of their presentations. Most people conclude but do not close. The close is what action you want your prospect to take as a result of your message. A conclusion is a wrap-up of what you just said. The reason many people don't close is based on the fear of hearing the word "no." Many believe when there is no close, neither is there any chance for rejection.

Delivering a persuasive presentation requires the ability to close. Remember to ask for the commitment; that's what you are there for. If you have been meeting with a great deal of clients but haven't been completing a great deal of transactions, ask yourself this, "Do I conclude, or do I close?" One generates action; the other gives your prospect a reason to stall.

Mistake Five–Wearing Inappropriate Dress

Are you making a fashion faux pas? Clients begin determining whether or not they like you within the first few seconds after you walk in the door, initially, based upon your dress. Although you haven't had time to talk about your company or product, they're already deciding if they will be doing business with you. Certain clothes are appropriate for the beach, and others are fine for a night on the town. Business attire is appropriate for giving presentations. These are not all one and the same!

Many of the industry books on dressing for success are outdated. I strongly recommend you meet with a clothing consultant at a major (reputable) department store for advice pertaining to color, style, and protocol for dress in varying presentations.

Mistake Six–Boring, Boring, Boring

Many professionals do not realize just how boring their presentations are—too many facts, the same old stories, a flat, boring, monotone voice. Sometimes professionals have been giving the same presentation for so long they just slip into autopilot. In today's competitive market, your presentations must be entertaining in order to obtain and maintain the attention of prospects.

Be creative! Put some energy into it! To stay sharp, practice with a tape recorder and listen to the playback to determine where your presentation begins to fall apart. Make improvements accordingly. Be sure to use material that is appropriate for the audience, whether the audience is made up of one or ten people.

Mistake Seven–Misusing The Allotted Time

I recently witnessed the president of a large publishing firm deliver brief overviews of the books in his new fall line. Each book was summed up in thirty seconds, and the meeting ended an hour early. He could have used the entire time more productively by building dazzling presentations on each book to inspire and excite the members of the sales team. The opposite can occur when a sales professional's presentation runs overtime; the prospect gets bored and tunes you out or is angry with your misuse of his/her time.

Determine how much time you have and develop a persuasive presentation that fits within those time parameters. In order to do this, you must practice your presentation in advance. You should be able to cover every important argument with an illustration, and know what to include and what to delete in case you are asked to shorten or lengthen the presentation at the last minute.

Mistake Eight–Overreliance On Visual Aids

If brochures, handouts, or slides could sell a product or service on their own, companies would not need salespeople. Depending too much on visual aids can give us a false sense of security. We tend to think it isn't necessary to prepare thoroughly because our props will lead us right through the presentation. We let the visual aid become the star and virtually run the show.

You are the star and the visual is the bit player! It's your job to bring the presentation to life. Strategically place visual aids in your presentation for emphasis of a major point or argument. You must practice with all handouts or aids to ensure that they enhance rather than detract from your presentation. Remember who's in charge–you are!

Mistake Nine–Exhibiting Distracting/Annoying Gestures

Your body naturally wants to gesture. Unfortunately, many times sales professionals don't realize the strange things their bodies are doing in the middle of a presentation before an important client. What you don't know can hurt you! Fidgeting with your tie, playing with your hair, clicking your pen, doodling, pacing, or other annoying behavior is very distracting and builds the image that you may be nervous versus confident and in control.

Seasoned pros know you have to practice in front of a mirror to be polished. Use a video camera to tape your presentation, and observe how you appear to your clients.

These nine points give you a brief overview of the most common mistakes salespeople make everyday in their presentations.

Such mistakes can cost you thousands of dollars every year in lost sales and commissions. Do a simple self-evaluation of your next presentation. Do you make any of these common mistakes when speaking to your clients and prospects? When you can identify the weaknesses in your presentation, you can begin to correct them. As a result, you will become more confident, more polished, more persuasive, and more consistent in delivering effective presentations.

Chapter 8

SALESpeak

Spotlight on
Women in Sales

Issues Rarely Discussed

In the course of attending my seminars, female participants frequently approach the podium and ask me what I think about the special challenges I face giving so many presentations. They want to know how I deal with borderline sexual harassment and discrimination—two obstacles that can affect income, not to mention self-esteem.

Knowing how to salvage a sale in a situation where these issues become apparent takes refined presentation and interpersonal skills. We need to be able to identify these obstacles, then overcome them. I am hesitant to offer the same road map to everyone because different people have vastly different values. I can describe a few common scenarios, however, and explain how other women handle them. At least there is comfort in knowing that we are not alone in facing these vexatious impediments to success.

Women Moving Into Sales

Today there are millions of successful American saleswomen, all of them giving one-on-one or group presentations. Some of these women make more than one million dollars annually.

Women are drawn to sales for many reasons other than the money. Some like the freedom associated with selling. Others like to ensure that their rewards equal their personal accomplishments. They want to be sure they are not held back from promotion because they are female, and they want to make sure they get equal pay for equal work.

According to *Telemarketing Magazine*, about 70 percent of all telemarketers working in the U.S. today are women. The challenges that face women today, whether in sales or other professions, come from several fronts. There are still closed-minded men who somehow, perhaps because they are lost in a time warp, think that the business world is a man's domain. They continue to try to perpetuate the "old-boys network." However, there are also plenty of women who would keep us from getting our rightful place in the sun.

There has always been gender competition, and there has always been competition between generations–for men too. There is competition between races, between religious groups, between ethnic groups, and between those coming up the ladder and those about to retire. Let's face it: the business world means competition, so we might as well get used to it.

Being Left Out

Knowing this, however, doesn't make it any less painful when we are carelessly left out of a group in which we should be included. When all the men in the organization go off to play golf, are you asked to go along? If not, how do you learn about the little bits of important inside information that get discussed? Do you only get them secondhand the following day? Accounts of this type of discrimination have been documented at length elsewhere, and I need not rehash what all of us know already.

Apart from the unpleasant recollections of such all-too-frequent cases of discrimination, I have found that the overwhelming

majority of men are supportive of women trying to better themselves and become more successful. Ironically, women attending
my seminars say that more often it is other *females* who attempt to
keep them from getting ahead. This contradicts much published
information about how women are now supposed to be supporting
each other.

All About Eve

During a discussion of this topic, a friend told me about a
film whose script focuses on this theme. I love to watch old
movies anyway, so I rented *All About Eve*. This 1950 classic with
Bette Davis and Anne Baxter won six Oscars, including Best
Picture. The film brilliantly depicts life in and around the theater,
with Davis playing an aging star who takes an admiring young
Baxter under her wing. Davis finds out too late that the younger
woman is literally taking over her life. Of course Baxter has all
the men in the story completely enraptured. The plot has Davis,
who tries to ease a younger woman's career path to the top,
being wickedly betrayed.

In today's competitive office environment, we can see how
only one experience of being undermined by another woman
may result in the *All About Eve* syndrome teaching us never to
trust an up-and-coming contender. Anyone following in our foot-
steps is likely to have an easier time than we did, anyway, just
because someone else already blazed the trail. Finding it remark-
ably easy to go so far so fast, a younger woman may be tempted
to encroach upon the territory of her mentor. Once this has
occurred, the mentor may try to thwart the younger woman's
efforts to get ahead.

Finally, any time the senior partner observes someone being
genuinely nice, she may assume, often falsely, that the younger
woman is out to get something. She may become so jealous of any
upwardly mobile female that she refuses to extend a hand—whether

it's deserved or not. A type of discrimination you may not be used to, this attitude from other women can be an obstacle some will encounter on the boulevard to success.

How Do I React?

When women encounter discrimination in the workplace, some withdraw and quietly swallow their pride. Others go ballistic. They get mad, they threaten, they file lawsuits, and generally create havoc. I suppose if you can afford the time and energy away from your primary task of earning a living or supporting a family, such reactions may be justifiable. But I believe there is a more effective way to deal with the problem—by being so persuasive and effective that no one can hold you back.

A friend in the computer business called on a company that expressed interest in buying her firm's software products. She arranged to give the interested company a presentation with two other members of her team, both men. The day before they were scheduled to appear, my friend's supervisor called her into his office and began to explain how conservative the management of the firm was they were about to visit. He suggested it might be more effective if one of the men—who was older and more experienced—gave the team presentation.

My friend conceded the lead position even though she had brought in the business and was the most qualified to give the presentation. She had been working with the clients and knew their requirements. The day of the meeting arrived, but the team faltered. The male employee who was leading had to keep turning to my friend for answers to questions. Finally she stepped in and took over, saving her more experienced associates the embarrassment of appearing ill-prepared. Together they made the sale, and her boss never again questioned her abilities.

Discrimination against women exists in a variety of forms, but it is just one more obstacle we need to overcome in order to make it to the top. In any case, you certainly can't let it throw you off track and affect your goals or your income. Instead, let its ugly face double your resolve to be the best that you can be.

Still Room For Femininity

If you find yourself in a situation in which you suspect you are dealing with a person or group who discriminates against women, don't try to compensate by concealing your femininity. You don't have to be androgynous in order to be successful. All you have to be is effective. The part of a woman's feminine nature that fosters humanistic values and shared responsibility can greatly enhance our working environments.

Should you be the victim of the *All About Eve* syndrome, the answer is not to be increasingly manipulative. The solution is to treat other women with loyalty and trust. If you know how to be persuasive through the use of logical, well-formulated arguments, you shouldn't need to resort to manipulative tactics. Despite the lyrics in Helen Reddy's song, "I am woman, hear me roar," you don't need to be roaring to be heard. Just refine your communication and presentation skills, and your increased credibility will overcome most problem situations.

▼

The part of a woman's feminine nature that fosters humanistic values and shared responsibility can greatly enhance our working environments.

▲

On Being Politically Correct

The question of gender issues in the workplace is one people feel uncomfortable about discussing. After my seminars, women approach me privately, troubled by men who have crossed the line into the area of harassment. The men express an interest in pursuing a personal, if not downright intimate, relationship when business is still on the table.

"My supervisor says just to tell them I'm not interested and move on," says one woman. Another protests, "My boss says, 'Just leave and don't do business with them,' but that's not always the right answer...." The reason it's not always the right answer is that leaving means you almost certainly won't make the sale! Sometimes you can't leave because you have to work side-by-side with the harassing individual.

The principal problem with direct or implied propositions for romantic liaisons, whether offered by a man to a woman or a woman to a man, is that the harassor may be in a temporary position of influence by the very nature of the sales relationship. Having the authority to purchase something from us, or to approve an idea we are presenting, he or she holds a degree of power over us. Although temporary, it is not unlike the authority held by someone in a corporate supervisory position. However, in that situation, there are laws governing an individual's conduct.

When you are in business and dynamically communicating your ideas in a strong way, people are attracted to you. You have

When you are in business and dynamically communicating your ideas in a strong way, people are attracted to you.

a product, service, opinion, or policy that you have packaged in a persuasive presentation. You are poised, you are prepared, and you are polished. During the presentation, you put out your best effort to impress and persuade. If you are enthusiastic, well dressed, and attractive, you have a powerful combination that will generate a lot of vitality.

Naturally, you are going to draw people to you, but women frequently don't anticipate the wide range of reactions they are likely to get. Sometimes that energy is translated by a male audience as sexual attraction, and men may make unwanted advances. "Wow! I was just presenting my sales pitch, and these guys thought I was selling something else entirely!" joked one of my clients. Many women don't have a clue about how to handle such situations.

Compromising Situations

....

There is a variety of responses you can use to manage these misdirected reactions. I will list a few that have been passed on to me by other women and some I have tried myself. Taking a snapshot of what you might encounter shows a fairly narrow range of challenges. On the one hand there is someone who really pushes himself (or herself) on you, creating a very uncomfortable situation. You need to realize that if someone makes an advance toward you that makes you feel uncomfortable or threatened in any way, you should immediately inform your supervisor. If you must keep working with the account, always bring a co-worker with you, preferably a person of the opposite sex. Under no circumstances should you allow a customer to place you in a physically or emotionally precarious situation.

Suggestive Remarks

....

The more common situations, however, are not threatening, just irritating. One problem with a customer who makes suggestive remarks is that he frequently won't come out and say what he really is proposing. Some men, particularly if they do it habitually, use subtle ways to suggest that a woman consider being intimate. "What does he really mean?" you ask yourself. Is he saying he wants to do business with me *and* that he would like to take me out? Or is he saying he wants to do business with me *if* he can take me out? Or maybe he is saying he just likes me on a personal level and would like to expand our business relationship to a personal level. Maybe he's just trying to entertain himself at my expense. Such men don't want to be accused of proposing something improper or offensive, but they continue to throw out their line with the hope of catching a fish.

Don't Overreact

....

This situation can be tricky for a woman, and sometimes can lead to inappropriate responses or hard feelings. After enough uncomfortable experiences, it is easy to overreact and interpret a rare and precious offer of genuine friendship as a disguised proposition. A male friend of mine once was deeply hurt. A woman he had been doing business with lost her job. He had come to care for her as a person, but, when he suggested they continue the friendship in spite of her layoff, she mistakenly assumed he was making a romantic advance. The unfortunate result was the end of a lovely friendship.

The Christmas Boat Parade

....

You can sometimes test whether people are coming on to you romantically or whether they merely wish to extend the hand of friendship. One of my seminar clients asked me to one of Southern California's festive events during the holidays. I wasn't sure whether he was asking me out on a date or if it was just his way of being friendly.

"Terri, we're all going out for dinner to watch the Christmas boat parade, and I was wondering if you would like to come with us...?" I hesitated for a moment. It sounded as if he were asking me on a date to a group event. It could also be his way of simply asking me to join his group of friends who were planning to go to the parade. Since I didn't really know what he meant, I asked him.

"Bill, is this a date—as in a romantic encounter—or is this a social invitation between friends of the opposite sex?" He laughed and assured me it was an invitation between friends. So I said, "Well, if it's an invitation between friends, I would love to go; but otherwise, I must tell you, I'm seeing someone right now, and I don't wish to confuse things by dating anyone else." This clarified for both of us exactly what type of invitation was on the table. It allowed me to get to know him better without jeopardizing my business relationship or networking contacts.

Nobility Can Be Costly

When the meaning is unclear, however, more often than not the message is just what it seems to be: a proposition. A friend recently told me about a sale she lost after her customer made several suggestions that she go out with him. Her first response was to try to ignore him, but that became impossible. Finally she said, "I must not be communicating my ideas on this proposal to you very effectively. If you would like, I would be happy to bring in my boss, John, and have him explain more clearly how our company can be of service to you."

In effect what she was saying was, "I'm not interested, and if you continue making sexual innuendoes, I'm going to turn this account over to my superior, who is a man. That way, this won't continue to be an issue." She finally left the client's office, somewhat abruptly, and the deal fell through. She was quite discouraged because she really wanted to get the account. It would have meant a large commission for her. She was disappointed that she had lost the business due to the client's being interested in her personally. Should she have done anything differently? Probably not, given her principles. She did what was correct, but she paid a high price, one that most people today can't afford. My feeling is she may have lost the sale, but she was true to herself.

Fighting Fire With Fire

Many women believe you have to fight fire with fire. They have a variety of techniques to keep this type of prospect interested in the negotiations underway, at least until they can complete the agreement. For a few, this involves calculated planning, for some it's merely a form of good-natured entertainment, and for others it's just another manageable challenge that comes with the territory.

Some women say they try to keep things light. They will joke around with a man, acknowledging his advances by saying, "Oh, how sweet," or "That's very charming," and not become offended. They follow with, "We're talking about business, and business is business. When we get finished, *then* we can talk about personal matters." In effect, the woman drags out the issue until *after* she completes the business agreement. Once that is wrapped up, she simply tells the man, "Thanks, but I'm not interested." Some women are able to use this approach to help further their business goals under some intense pressure. Several men I know have told me that they admire a woman who can tactfully control their customers' priorities!

▼

If you go with the flow, you can wind up losing the business because you have a personal relationship with your client.

▲

Another approach, at least for a single woman, is to "go with the flow." She may date the prospect, just having a good time. She remains open the entire time negotiations are underway. She may not yet know whether she likes the man because she really doesn't have enough information. Women have told me some of their best times—and best friends—have resulted from these escapades. No matter which course you follow, however, there is a risk. If you go with the flow, you can wind up losing the business *because* you have a personal relationship with your client.

Managing Unwanted Advances

Kathy, who is vice-president of a title company, is one of the best examples I know of a woman who has learned how to deal effectively with men's amorous advances. Young and extremely attractive, she combines an enthusiastic and confident personality with a polished presentation. She impresses both men and women in the audience. She is constantly being approached by men who want to ask her out and has had countless offers. Following her presentations, she has received everything from flowers to invitations for dinner, and some of these advances have been quite bold. While to some of us this may sound like a dream come true, it isn't fun when it compromises your business.

The technique that Kathy has perfected is successful in preventing her from losing business even when someone makes an audacious pass at her. First, she believes it isn't necessary, and it certainly isn't profitable, to hurt a man's pride while managing his uninvited flirtations.

When she was single, Kathy's attitude was to deal with each proposal on a case-by-case basis. Of course, 99 percent of the time, she wasn't the least bit interested. She handled the proposition by saying, "Thank you *so* much; I'm very flattered. Actually, I'm quite involved with someone right now and am head over heels in love with him, but yes, if something ever happens, and I'm no longer seeing him, believe me, you will be the first person I call." That's not a definite "no," but it sure puts the man in a permanent holding pattern!

Now that she is married, Kathy says, "Wow, if I weren't married I would be knocking down your door," adding immediately, "I think that you are such a super guy... I've been wracking my brain trying to think of which friend I have that I could fix you up with."

When The Feeling Is Mutual

At some point, you may discover you are very attracted to a man with whom you do business. Perhaps the best approach here is to be completely honest with each other about what's happening, then try to manage the situation together. You will still have a far better chance of responsibly representing the economic interests of both yourself and your employer if you complete all business *before* you begin any type of romantic relationship. If his is an ongoing account, you can ask your supervisor to have it transferred to a colleague.

Just One More Objection

While delivering powerful, persuasive presentations can dramatically affect your income and your career, in your rise to the top, you may run into the twin sisters of harassment and discrimination. Think of each instance as just another problem to be overcome on the road toward convincing your audience or closing the sale. With forethought and the use of your persuasive tool kit, you can successfully manage even these thorny obstacles.

Chapter 9

SALESpeak

Conclusion

Summary

In the preceding pages, I have given you a wealth of information to help you deliver more persuasive presentations. Let's review several key areas we have covered.

Learned Skill

First it is important to remember that being a powerful and persuasive speaker is a learned skill. Although many people have a fear of public speaking, all people are engaged in this activity. When we realize that a speech can be presented to one or one hundred people, we tend to understand better why our presentations to individual clients or prospects are really examples of public speaking. To be a great salesperson, one must be a great public speaker, even if each sale is to a single individual.

Sharpening presentation skills should be a lifelong process for the professional. Possessing skills of persuasion will be a necessity during the lean era

▼

To be a great salesperson, one must be a great public speaker, even if each sale is to a single individual.

▲

of the 1990s. With the ability to persuade effectively, we can dramatically enhance our careers and our personal lives.

Being effective persuaders means communicating our sincerity, our enthusiasm, and even our passion. We realize that products often are similar, so people buy people. We must convince our clients that we are sincerely interested in meeting their needs. When giving a business presentation, we must deliver a speech that comes from the heart if we expect an individual or group to act on our recommendations.

New Sales Model

To respond to the challenging marketplace of the 1990s, we have developed the inverted pyramid circle model for sales calls. Our clients are searching for value more than ever before and frequently will check between three and five competitors before making a purchase decision. The inverted pyramid circle stresses the need for a logical but memorable sales presentation. To complete the sale, it relies on the salesperson's effective expression of his or her personality.

Listening is an essential skill for the sales professional and occupies much of the time spent selling or persuasively presenting. Unfortunately, many of us don't listen very well, which affects our bottom line. Our prospects will better retain the information we provide them if they understand it. We have to listen to their questions to know whether or not they do. The better we listen, the more involved we can be and the more we can influence the outcome of the sales call.

A good presentation may result in closing a sale, but it also may create other opportunities at the same time. Even in short talks, you should never underestimate the power of your presentation. Because the potential can be unknown—little fish have a way of traveling with big fish—you should always prepare adequately for your presentations.

Persuasive Versus Informative

For others there are different types of talks, but for the sales professional, there is only one—persuasive. While others may find an appropriate opportunity to give an informative presentation, it should not be an option for the salesperson. In order to be persuasive, you will have to call upon your client to act. You will be more effective and less stressed if you are persuasive throughout your presentation than if you wait until the end when you close. Spreading out your persuasive arguments helps relieve what we call communication apprehension. There are several distinct parts to a persuasive presentation. The key to employing them effectively is to plan your talk with an outline.

> ▼
> In order to be an effective persuasive speaker you will have to commit to excellence and the work it takes to achieve it.
> ▲

In order to be an effective persuasive speaker you will have to commit to excellence and the work it takes to achieve it. You will have to learn to be a "spy" and do research on your competition. Finding out if your customer uses your competition—and more importantly, why—can help target your efforts. Similarly, you should spend time getting to know your audience. Doing some homework on your clients' personal and business tastes often pays off handsomely. By objectively comparing your products and services to those of your competitor in a competitive analysis, you can identify areas where you may need to improve as well as discover ideas for change.

Obtaining Credibility

One of our main objectives is to obtain credibility. To this end we use speech supports such as statistics, anecdotes, analogies, and examples. These also make our talks more entertaining and memorable. Tying our anecdotes to a client's emotional needs can be powerfully persuasive. Where do we get anecdotes and examples? Personal experience, books, shows, and other people provide them.

In Chapter Six, we enumerated the steps involved in organizing a presentation from scratch. We discussed signposting and transitions as well as the development of points in the body of the speech leading to the conclusion and close. We provided you with an outline form for practicing a persuasive presentation that you can copy and use. We addressed how to handle it when the boss asks you to prepare a presentation overnight. We also gave you a list of twenty-one keys to use in determining how to prepare your talk.

Taking Risks

In Chapter Seven we put it all together and talked about how it feels to get out in front of an individual or group and carry the full burden of a formal presentation. There is a risk involved in putting yourself on the line, but there are significant rewards as well. We discussed the signs and causes of nervousness and how to handle anxiety. Becoming a power speaker involves acquiring polish. The keys to becoming polished include knowledge, practice, and the will to improve. We gave you a few tips on appropriate dress and body language, and several do's and don'ts when you are giving your presentation.

Having these skills can make the difference between being highly successful in your career and being only marginal. However, there are several underlying values and beliefs you must also have in order to be a successful sales professional and power speaker.

To be successful, you must know what you want to do. You must recognize that there is a price to success and you must resolve to pay it. Literally, you must choose to be a success for it to happen. I believe there are basically two types of people in the world—choosers and excusers.

Which One Are You?

....

Choosers accept accountability for everything they say or think. Excusers look for excuses by blaming circumstances or other people. Can you identify the excusers in your office? Choosers look for solutions while excusers see only problems. Choosers will keep on trying in the face of challenging situations, but excusers will blame the market. Choosers will work to overcome circumstances while excusers become victims of circumstances. Choosers realize that the power to choose is one of their greatest powers. Excusers think they can't control the future so they don't try.

Choosers:

1. Accept accountability for everything they do, say, or think
2. Look for solutions
3. Keep on trying in the face of challenging situations
4. Work to overcome circumstances
5. Know the power to choose is one of the greatest gifts and plan to use it wisely

Excusers:

1. Look for excuses by blaming circumstances on other people
2. See problems
3. Blame the market
4. Are victims of circumstances
5. Think they can't control their future, so they don't try

Pick Your Category

....

One of my early sales managers took me aside one day during training and told me a truism that I think about often. He said,

"Terri Lynn, there are three types of people in the world—those who make things happen, those who watch things happen, and those who say, 'Whoa, what happened?'" Decide which one of these you are and which one you want to be. From my observations, the people who make things happen have a lot more fun in life.

> ▼
> Remember that of all the variables in business, the one thing you can control is your public speaking ability.
> ▲

Remember that of all the variables in business, the one thing you can control is your public speaking ability. This skill can open doors for you that are closed to the average person. In order to be the best speaker you can be, you have to instill your presentations with passion and sincerity.

You Are A Living Example

The story I recounted in the introduction about gaining access to a residential real estate organization by presenting the president with a white rose is more than just an anecdote on the importance of novel approaches. It is about making people feel special. When you are original, sincere, and credible, you bestow on people the caring respect they deserve as individuals. To be a living example of that message in today's fast-paced and sometimes unfeeling business environment will be to help create the kind of world that we can take pride in passing on to our children.

Sjodin Communications Information Request Form

■ For information on how Sjodin Communications may be of service to you, your company, or professional organization, please write to:

SJODIN COMMUNICATIONS
P.O. Box 8998
Fountain Valley, CA 92728-8998
Or call:
SJODIN COMMUNICATIONS (714) 540-5594

Yes, I have read *"SALESpeak: Everybody Sells Something."*
Please send me information on:
❑ Obtaining Terri Sjodin for a speaking engagement
❑ In-house Video Taping Workshop

NAME: _____
COMPANY: _____
POSITION: _____
ADDRESS:_____
CITY: _____ STATE: _____ ZIP: _____
BUSINESS PHONE: (   )_____

Please provide us with a brief description of the kind of products or services your company sells.

_____
_____
_____
_____